MAKING SHIPWRECK OF THE FAITH

Evangelicals and Roman Catholics Together

Kevin Reed

MAKING SHIPWRECK OF THE FAITH

Evangelicals and

Roman Catholics Together

Kevin Reed

Holding faith, and a good conscience;
which some having put away
concerning faith have
made shipwreck.

1 Timothy 1:19

Protestant Heritage Press
P. O. Box 180922
Dallas, Texas 75218

Some of the material in chapter 3 is adapted from the expanded treatment of the subject in *Biblical Worship* by Kevin Reed (Dallas: Presbyterian Heritage Publications, 1995).

Contents

Chapter 1

Introduction

In 1994, a group of notable evangelicals and Roman Catholics issued a statement of cooperation entitled, "Evangelicals and Catholics Together: The Christian Mission in the Third Millennium." The document has provoked numerous articles and books assailing the evangelical signatories to the accord.

The present author has surveyed many of the responses to ECT, but he has come away with mixed feelings. So far, most of the critics of ECT take aim at areas where Rome is an easy target; but they avoid critical aspects of doctrine and practice where modern evangelicals exhibit remarkable similarities to Rome.

There can be no question that the ECT document represents a colossal compromise with Rome on the part of any professing Protestant who supports it. Moreover, the accord and its aftermath reveal much about the present state of evangelicalism. In particular, the situation demonstrates that most evangelicals have departed from the doctrines and practices of the Protestant Reformation.

We take this opportunity to focus upon the preeminent issues of the Reformation. The present essay seeks to redirect the focus of readers to the bigger picture, providing a framework for assessing Roman Catholicism, contemporary evangelicalism, and the ECT document. This book illustrates how both Romanists and evangelicals have rejected scriptural teaching about (1.) the essence of the gospel, (2.) divinely-instituted worship, and (3.) the marks of a true church. By corrupting the gospel, worship, and the church, evangelicals and Roman Catholics together are making shipwreck of the Christian faith.

Our study will mention some of the specious beliefs and practices of both Roman Catholics and evangelicals. When confronted with the unbiblical practices of Rome, Protestants often assume that there is a prior misunderstanding of doctrine which leads to a corresponding corruption in practice. Protestant theology moves from thought to practice, so that is the way Protestants tend to analyze the religion of others. Yet, this reasoning (from anterior belief to posterior practice) does not always apply to Roman Catholicism; and it is increasingly unserviceable when dealing with evangelicals. The fact is, aberrant practices often obtain admission and long usage in religious assemblies before anyone seeks to provide a rationale for them. When a practice is subsequently questioned, latter-day apologists scurry to devise a justification for their actions. This *ex post facto* method of building a rationale is what leads to some of the bizarre scripture-twisting so prevalent in Rome and modern evangelicalism.[1]

As our analysis proceeds, we will criticize some of the established doctrines and practices of both Romanists and evangelicals. It is not our desire to create animosity, but our commitment to *sola scriptura* requires that we candidly examine the beliefs and practices of all parties in this controversy.

The sober reality is that ECT is merely the tip of the iceberg. Both Roman Catholics and evangelicals are making shipwreck of the faith. If there is going to be a recovery of biblical religion in our land, we must repent and return to the scriptural principles which marked the Protestant Reformation.

---

1. See the comments by Richard Whately, cited by William Cunningham, "The Errors of Romanism," in *Discussions on Church Principles: Popish, Erastian, and Presbyterian* (1863; rpt. Edmonton: Still Waters Revival Books, 1991), pp. 15-18.

Chapter 2

The Way of Salvation

At the heart of the controversy between Rome and historic Protestants is a dispute over the way of salvation. In speaking of salvation, we note that the term "salvation" encompasses a wide range of important topics, and it is important to distinguish between various aspects of redemption.

Since the fall of mankind, the human race stands in need of salvation (or deliverance): deliverance from the *guilt* of sin, and also deliverance from the *power* of sin. From the biblical doctrine of *justification,* we learn the divine provision whereby sinners are delivered from the *punishment* due to the guilt of their sins. From the doctrine of *sanctification,* we learn the means whereby God delivers sinners from the reigning *power* of sin.

Of course, there are other facets of redemption, such as election, effectual calling, glorification, etc. Obviously the subjects of redemption are interrelated to one another; but they are not identical, and should not be confounded. Even though the various aspects of salvation bear a close relationship to one another, the scriptures clearly distinguish between them. In several places within Paul's epistles, the apostle maintains a clear distinction between justification and sanctification. For example: "But ye are washed, but ye are sanctified, but ye are justified in the name of the Lord Jesus, and by the Spirit of our God" (1 Cor. 6:11; cf. Rom. 8:30; 1 Cor. 1:30).[1]

---

1. "*Wherein do justification and sanctification differ?* Although sanctification be inseparably joined with justification, yet they differ, in that God in justification imputeth the righteousness of Christ; in sanctification his Spirit infuseth grace, and enableth to the exercise thereof; in the former, sin is

Another closely related topic is the nature of *regeneration,* or the new birth. Those whom God regenerates are given repentance, faith, and inward renewal so that they strive for godliness.

With the foregoing considerations in view, we wish to assert several important truths which bear on the state of Roman Catholicism and modern evangelicalism.

Justification

Centuries ago, the patriarch Job exclaimed, "How should man be just with God? ... For he is not a man, as I am, that I should answer him, and we should come together in judgment. Neither is there any daysman betwixt us, that might lay his hand upon us both" (Job 9:1, 32-33). Even so, Job later expressed the sublime confidence of resting in his redeemer: "For I know that my redeemer liveth, and that he shall stand at the latter day upon the earth; and though after my skin worms destroy this body, yet in my flesh shall I see God: whom I shall see for myself, and mine eyes shall behold, and not another" (Job 19:25-27).

The utterances of the patriarch illustrate well both the need for, and the sufficiency of, the work of our redeemer, Christ Jesus. Whereas no ordinary man could act as our mediator, yet there is good news of redemption: "there is one God, and one mediator between God and men, the man Christ Jesus; who gave himself a ransom.... God was manifest in the flesh" (1 Tim. 2:5-6, 3:16).

A crucial question every man must ponder is how he can be *just* before God. This is a *legal* question, pertaining to our *guilt* as sinners. We are all guilty; there can be no denial of that fact. "There is none righteous, no, not one" (Rom. 3:10). We have nothing of merit to bring before God to improve our standing, for "we are all as an unclean thing, and all our righteousnesses are as filthy rags" (Isa. 64:6). If we remain in this guilty state, we must suffer the

---

pardoned; in the other, it is subdued: the one doth equally free all believers from the revenging wrath of God, and that perfectly in this life, that they never fall into condemnation; the other is neither equal in all, nor in this life perfect in any, but growing up to perfection." Westminster Larger Catechism, #77.

punishment due for our sins, which is everlasting torment in hell. Truly our case is desperate.

Moreover, we need more than forgiveness for the guilt of sins committed. If we would appear before the holy LORD of glory, we need a *positive righteousness,* not just a pardon for our offenses. Thus the case is clear: if we are to stand just (or righteous) before God, we must obtain righteousness from a source outside ourselves.

Let us, then, give praise unto God: through his wondrous plan of redemption, such a righteousness is found in Christ! In Christ alone may we find the righteousness we inherently lack. "For he hath made him to be sin for us, who knew no sin; that we might be made the righteousness of God in him." He "was delivered for our offences, and was raised again for our justification" (2 Cor. 5:21; Rom. 4:25). Thus is he called, "The LORD our righteousness" (Jer. 23:6; 33:16).

Christ Jesus provides the *sole ground* of righteousness for redeemed sinners. "When he had *by himself* purged our sins, sat down on the right hand of the Majesty on high" (Heb. 1:3).

This truth is at the foundation of historic Protestant theology; hence the slogan, "*Solus Christus!*" The Westminster Shorter Catechism (#33) summarizes: "Justification is an act of God's free grace, wherein he pardoneth all our sins, and accepteth us as righteous in his sight, *only for the righteousness of Christ imputed to us....*"

Essentially, then, justification is a forensic (or legal) concept. The sinner is declared righteous, based solely upon the righteousness of another, even Christ Jesus. The righteousness of Christ is the ground of salvation.

Human Depravity

We have already spoken of the remedy for the guilt of sin. But mankind has another problem as well. Since the fall of Adam, every human being born by ordinary generation has inherited a *corrupt nature,* an evil heart.

The Bible is absolutely clear about the wicked nature of mankind. Men are *totally unwilling* to seek God; their wills are wholly inclined to evil. "There is none that seeketh after God." "The carnal mind is enmity against God" (Rom. 3:11; 8:7). The human will is not free, precisely because it is enslaved to evil. While men are able to choose from a range of different actions, their native power to choose righteousness was lost at the fall.

Moreover, even if men were inclined to seek God, their understanding is so darkened that they cannot grasp the truth of God: "there is none that understandeth." "The natural man receiveth not the things of the Spirit of God: for they are foolishness unto him: neither can he know them, because they are spiritually discerned" (Rom. 3:11; 1 Cor. 2:14).

Men are inherently incapable of contributing anything favourable to God, for "there is none that doeth good, no, not one" (Rom. 3:12). "Can the Ethiopian change his skin, or the leopard his spots? then may ye also do good, that are accustomed to do evil. " (Jer. 13:23).

There is a simple explanation for this total inability on the part of mankind. Natural men are spiritually *dead,* "dead in trespasses and sins" (Eph. 2:1), wholly incapable of the motions of living creatures. They can neither perceive, understand, nor respond to the spiritual verities which surround them. These dead men need life, spiritual life; they need to be "born again" – born spiritually.

Regeneration

Earlier we mentioned *regeneration,* or the new birth. The expression "born again" has been bantered about prominently within "evangelical" circles in recent years, but the terminology is often employed without adequate definition. Yet, a mistake regarding the nature of regeneration can be critical, resulting in a horrendous distortion of the doctrine of salvation.

The Second Helvetic Confession describes the new birth in the following manner: "In regeneration the understanding is illuminated by the Holy Spirit, that it may understand both the mysteries and will of God. And the will itself is not only changed by the Spirit, but it is also endued with faculties, that, of its own accord, it may both will and do good."[2]

Among the fruits of regeneration are *faith* and *repentance.* These graces are the results of God's work within the sinner; *they are not the cause of the new birth.* The inherent state of mankind is rebellion against God – enmity, ignorance, and unbelief. In order for sinners to exercise faith and repentance, the Spirit of God must convince us of our sin and misery, enlighten our minds in the knowledge of Christ, renew our wills, and persuade and enable us to embrace Jesus Christ as he is freely offered in the gospel.[3]

Unlike the imputed righteousness of Christ, which is *external* to the sinner, faith and repentance are the works of God *within* the sinner. Nevertheless, these *internal* works are totally gracious, in no way flowing from the actions, merit or the ability of the redeemed sinner.

Scripture teaches that salvation is "by grace ... through faith; and that not of yourselves: it is the gift of God: not of works, lest any man should boast" (Eph. 2:8-9). Thus, *even faith is a gift;* faith is not an action taken by the sinner of his own innate ability. Salvation is "not of him that willeth, nor of him that runneth, but of God that showeth mercy" (Rom. 9:16). The empowerment is sovereignly granted by the Spirit of God. "But as many as received him, to them gave he power to become the sons of God, even to them that believe on his name: which were born, not of blood, *nor of the will of the flesh, nor of the will of man,* but of God" (John 1:12-13; cf. 3:6-8).

Justification by Faith

We now move to the relationship between justification and faith. Simply stated: faith is God's appointed instrument whereby the

2. Second Helvetic Confession, Chapter 9. The English translation here is taken from Philip Schaff, *The Creeds of Christendom,* 6th edition (1931; rpt. Grand Rapids: Baker, 1983), vol. 3, p. 846. For proof of the definition, the confession cites Jer. 31:33, Ezek. 36:27, John 8:36, Phil. 1:29; 2:13.

3. Cf. Westminster Shorter Catechism #31.

sinner receives justification. Faith is not the ground of justification, for the only ground of justification is the imputed righteousness of Christ.[4] The Westminster Shorter Catechism (#33) states this doctrine well: "Justification is an act of God's free grace, wherein he pardoneth all our sins, and accepteth us as righteous in his sight, only for the righteousness of Christ imputed to us, and *received by faith alone.*" We can see this principle in the text already referenced, "For by grace are ye saved through faith; and that not of yourselves: it is the gift of God: not of works, lest any man should boast" (Ephesians 2:8-9).

Moreover, the doctrine is asserted from the example of Abraham, "he believed in the LORD; and he counted it to him for righteousness" (Gen. 15:6). Abraham's faith is expounded by Paul in Romans 4:2-5: "If Abraham were justified by works, he hath whereof to glory; but not before God. For what saith the scripture? Abraham believed God, and it was counted unto him for righteousness. Now to him that worketh is the reward not reckoned of grace, but of debt. But to him that worketh not, but believeth on him that justifieth the ungodly, his faith is counted for righteousness."

Saving Faith

We cannot leave this discussion without considering the nature of saving faith. The term *faith* needs to be defined by its scriptural use. In the language of the New Testament, the noun form is *faith,* the verb form is *believe.*

In biblical terminology, the word *believe* means much more than *mental assent.* Saving faith is more than a bare acknowledgment of a few historical facts about Jesus of Nazareth. After all, "the devils also believe, and tremble" (James 2:19). Theologians have often referred to this belief as *historic faith,* in order to distinguish it from saving faith.[5]

4. For an excellent discussion on the role of faith, see Joel R. Beeke, "Justification by Faith Alone (The Relation of Faith to Justification)," chapter 3 of *Justification by Faith Alone* (edited by Don Kistler; Morgan, Pa.: Soli Deo Gloria, 1994), pp. 53-105.

The Bible also describes a *temporary faith:* an inadequate belief which is illustrated in the parable of the soils. Some people hear the word of God, "which, when they hear, receive the word with joy; and these have no root, which for a while believe, and in time of temptation fall away" (Luke 8:13).[6]

As noted, the patriarch Abraham is held forth in scriptures as an example of *saving faith.* Abraham not only believed God, but he trusted in the promises of God, resting upon the Lord alone as his redeemer. As Jesus declared, "Your father Abraham rejoiced to see my day: and he saw it, and was glad" (John 8:56).

Historic Protestants have given a clear testimony about the nature of saving faith. "Faith in Jesus Christ is a saving grace, whereby we receive and rest upon him alone, as he is offered in the gospel."[7]

This definition preserves the distinctive quality of *trust* ("receive and rest upon him alone"), which is an essential aspect of genuine faith. Likewise, this description points to another critical aspect of faith: the *content* of our belief. We must rely upon the Christ of the scriptures, not an imaginary Christ made to suit the fancies of men.

It makes little sense to profess belief in Jesus of Nazareth, if we then discard the biblical teaching concerning him. Yet, that is precisely what multitudes have done throughout the centuries: they embrace heretical notions about Jesus, thereby resting in "cunningly devised fables" (2 Pet. 1:16), rather than exercising true faith in the Christ of the Bible.

For example, Jehovah's Witnesses, following the Arians of old, deny the deity of Christ, imagining him to be merely a created

---

5. For an example of a standard exposition on different kinds of faith, see Thomas Manton, "Faith," in *A Body of Divinity* (1692; rpt. Edinburgh: Banner of Truth, 1992), pp. 215-20.

6. There are other forms of inadequate faith illustrated in scripture, such as the superficial belief of people who witnessed miracles, acknowledged the supernatural elements they saw, but yet lacked a genuine faith in Christ (cf. Acts 8:13, 21-23).

7. Westminster Shorter Catechism #86.

being. Similarly, Mormons, by exalting humanity, deny the uniqueness of Christ's person, by asserting the divinity of all mankind. These are "damnable heresies" (2 Pet. 2:1), revealing the corrupt "faith" of the adherents to these false religions.

Regarding his person, our Lord himself declared, "If ye believe not that I am he, ye shall die in your sins.... Before Abraham was, I am" (John 8:24, 58). By using the covenant name of God (cf. Ex. 3:14), and applying it unto himself in this context, Jesus clearly indicates that belief in his deity is a fundamental component of saving faith.

If it is essential for us to rest upon Christ alone "as he is offered to us in the gospel," then it is necessary for us to know and embrace the truths concerning him in the scriptures. For "faith cometh by hearing, and hearing by the word of God." (Rom. 10:17).

How is Christ presented in the gospel? Reformation preachers enunciated the biblical teaching that "Christ, as our redeemer, executes the office of a prophet, of a priest, and of a king."[8] As the consummate prophet, Jesus reveals to us the very being of God, and the way of salvation (John 1:18). As priest, Christ "was once offered to bear the sins of many," "to make reconciliation for the sins of the people" (Heb. 9:28, 2:17). He is *the Lord* Jesus Christ, and he will reign "till he hath put all enemies under his feet" (1 Cor. 15:25). Any presentation which neglects, distorts, or denies these truths regarding Christ is not biblical preaching; it will leave hearers in danger of believing in a false Christ.

The Relationship Between Faith and Works

In defending the doctrine of justification by faith alone, we stated that the sinner's faith is the gift of God – the fruit of regeneration. Likewise, when the Spirit of God regenerates a man, the man's inner being is transformed. "Therefore if any man be in Christ, he is a new creature: old things are passed away; behold, all things are become new" (2 Cor. 5:17). The redeemed sinner is progres-

---

8. Westminster Shorter Catechism # 23.

sively renewed after the image of God, "in righteousness and true holiness" (Eph. 4:24). Thus, the true believer will exhibit a change of heart by his good works.

Saving faith inevitably leads to good works. Note the relationship between faith and works in God's redemptive design. "For by grace are ye saved *through faith;* and that not of yourselves: it is the gift of God: not of works, lest any man should boast. *For we are his workmanship, created in Christ Jesus unto good works,* which God hath before ordained that we should walk in them" (Eph. 2:8-10).

As noted earlier, justification should not be confounded with sanctification; but neither should it be divorced from sanctification, as if redemption involves one to the exclusion of the other.[9] The redeemed sinner's deliverance from the guilt of sin evokes a desire to be free from the power of sin as well. Therefore, the genuine believer pursues "holiness, without which no man shall see the Lord" (Heb. 12:14).

Fatal Errors of Roman Catholicism

The foregoing presentation is only a cursory reminder of major truths connected with the doctrine of salvation. Nevertheless, the issues raised provide a basis for evaluating both Roman Catholicism and contemporary evangelicalism.

With reference to Rome, we may note several fatal deviations from biblical teaching.

1. Rome explicitly denies the doctrine of justification by faith alone, pronouncing an anathema upon those who hold to this principle. The 9th canon of the Council of Trent says: "If any one saith, that by faith alone the impious is justified, in such wise as to mean, that nothing else is required to cooperate in order to the obtaining the grace of Justification, and that it is not in any way necessary, that he be prepared and disposed by the movement of his own will: let him be anathema."[10]

---

9. See note 1 above.

10. Cited from Schaff, *Creeds of Christendom,* vol. 2, p. 112.

Many of Trent's other anathemas are hurled at caricatures of Protestants, while some of the denunciations are directed toward heresies which Protestants themselves abhor. Regardless of the "straw men" that Trent created to serve as a target, it is absolutely clear that the council (and thereby the Romish church) rejected the call of Protestants to embrace the biblical doctrine of justification by faith. This fact has been made the subject of so much discussion, both historically and recently, that we shall not dwell on it here.[11]

2. Rome has corrupted the gospel by confounding justification and sanctification. Justification is viewed as a process, begun at baptism, in which the sinner becomes righteous through *infused grace.* According to Trent, "That justice which is called ours, because that we are justified from its being inherent in us, that same is (the justice) of God, because that it is infused into us of God, through the merit of Christ."[12] In other words, the forensic nature of justification is jettisoned. The imputed righteousness of Christ is not sought; instead, an inherent righteousness is required for the sinner to improve his state of justification.

Roman Catholics speak of faith and grace in relation to justification. To the casual non-Romanist, this may sound very similar to the words used by Protestants. But when one begins to examine how the terms are defined, and the relationship they bear to one another, radical differences become apparent.[13]

---

11. Doctrinal statements regarding justification can be found in the Protestant creeds, the writings of the reformers, and Puritan sermons. Historic surveys on justification may be found in James Buchanan, *The Doctrine of Justification: An Outline of Its History in the Church and of Its Exposition from Scripture* (Edinburgh, 1867) and William Cunningham, "Justification," Chapter 21 of *Historical Theology* (1862; rpt. Edinburgh: Banner of Truth, 1979), vol. 2, pp. 1-120. Recent treatments of the subject may be found within the following works: Don Kistler, ed., *Justification by Faith Alone* (Morgan, Pa.: Soli Deo Gloria, 1995); John MacArthur, *Reckless Faith: When the Church Loses Its Will to Discern* (Wheaton: Crossway Books, 1994).

12. Council of Trent, "Decree on Justification," chapter 16; cited from Schaff, *Creeds of Christendom,* vol. 2, pp. 108-09.

Since Romanists view justification as a process within a man, they go on to assert that Christians, "through the observance of the commandments of God and of the Church, faith co-operating with good works, increase in that justice which they have received through the grace of Christ, and are still further justified."[14]

Underlying this Romish view of salvation is a faulty view of the inherent state of fallen mankind. While Romanists will acknowledge that mankind was damaged at the fall of Adam, the Romish system of salvation is a practical denial of the inherent inability of men to contribute to their redemption.

We have previously shown that the unregenerate man is ignorant, unwilling, and incapable of contributing to his salvation. Yet, to speak of man's "faith co-operating with good works," as a factor in justification, is to make man a partial saviour of himself. In practical terms, this constitutes a works righteousness. "For

---

13. "That a sinner may be saved, the scriptures declare that he must be both justified and sanctified: the Romanists, as if one of those were by requisite, call that 'justification,' which in scripture is 'sanctification;' and that which in scripture is "justification," they admit not, as distinct from inherent righteousness.

"The apostle Paul, who most insists upon the doctrine of justification, delivers these two as distinct things, (1 Cor. 6:11, and elsewhere). He ascribes justification commonly to the blood of Christ (as in the text [Rom. 3:24], and Rom. 5:8-9); sanctification to the Spirit of Christ (Titus 3:5).

"However, the Papists' promiscuous use of words might be tolerated, if they did not confound the things, and contend that we are formally justified by that which is the form and essence of sanctification, namely, inherent righteousness. The danger is that which the apostle would have the Jews avoid, when he expresseth his hearty desire that they might be saved: 'For they being ignorant of God's righteousness, and going about to establish their own righteousness, have not submitted themselves unto the righteousness of God' (Rom. 10:3)." David Clarkson, "The Doctrine of Justification is Dangerously Corrupted in the Roman Church," in *Select Works of the Reverend and Learned David Clarkson* (1675; London [Wycliffe Society], 1846), p. 472.

14. Council of Trent, "Decree on Justification," chapter 10; cited from Schaff, *Creeds of Christendom*, vol. 2, p. 99.

they being ignorant of God's righteousness, and going about to establish their own righteousness, have not submitted themselves unto the righteousness of God" (Rom. 10:3).

This perversion of the doctrine of salvation (by Rome) has been widely documented. We will not dwell on it here, but merely remind our readers of this fatal corruption of the gospel.[15]

3. Rome teaches that grace is obtained through the sacraments: that is, the process of "justification" is furthered by performance of the rites of the church. In the Romish system of salvation, grace is mediated through the Church via the sacraments. Hence the followers of Rome depend upon the rituals of the church in their redemption.

The Council of Trent speaks of "the most holy sacraments of the church, through which all true justice either begins, or being begun is increased, or being lost is repaired."[16] This is the essence of sacerdotalism.

Baptismal regeneration is asserted, for Trent claims that the merit of Christ "is applied, both to adults and to infants, by the sacrament of baptism."[17] The assertion is made that, through baptism, the original sin of Adam is taken away and remission is granted for all sins which have been committed prior to baptism. After baptism, a man may fall from the state of justification; in that case, he may seek restoration through the sacrament of penance.[18]

In this sacerdotal system, adherents can never really obtain assurance of final salvation or perseverance. Therefore, they seek to increase their justice through the sacrament of the eucharist (the Mass). Based on the doctrine of transubstantiation, the Mass

---

15. See notes 11 and 13 above.

16. Council of Trent, "Decree on the Sacraments." Cited from Schaff, *Creeds of Christendom,* vol. 2, p. 118.

17. Council of Trent, "Decree on Original Sin," section 3. Cited from Schaff, *Creeds of Christendom,* vol. 2, p. 86.

18. See Council of Trent, "Decree on Justification," sections 3-4, 14. In Schaff, *Creeds of Christendom,* vol. 2, p. 90-91, 104-05.

is held forth as an actual resacrifice of Christ, possessing propitiatory merits which are dispensed by the church to the living and the dead.[19]

Thus, while Romanists claim that salvation comes from God, they contend that saving grace is channeled through the rites of the church. The ultimate effect of Rome's sacerdotalism is to make the institutional church the mediator between God and man; the church and her priests usurp the role of Christ.

From the foregoing discussion, it should be clear that Roman Catholicism has exchanged the biblical gospel for another gospel. The Romish Church has denied the forensic nature of justification; it has rejected the scriptural teaching of justification by faith; it has confounded justification and sanctification; they have sought regeneration by the performance of ecclesiastical rites.

Fatal Errors of Contemporary Evangelicalism

We've noted some of the fatal flaws of Roman Catholicism. But our examination of the issues cannot stop with Rome; modern evangelicals also subvert the doctrine of salvation by grace.

If Rome is denounced for its doctrine of baptismal regeneration, then contemporary evangelicalism must be criticized for its practice of *decisional regeneration.* This error may take two prominent forms: (1.) mass meetings where hearers are asked to come forward at the "invitation" (or altar call) in order to register their decision for Christ (an action often equated with faith or regeneration); and (2.) the one-on-one method of Pelagian evangelism where the "convert" is told to recite a "sinner's prayer," after which he is solemnly assured of his salvation and exhorted not to doubt his favourable standing before God. (No doctrine of papal absolution was ever stated with more certainty). Both of these methods exhibit a complete misunderstanding of the biblical way of salvation.

---

19. See Council of Trent, "Doctrine on the Sacrifice of the Mass," section 2 In Schaff, *Creeds of Christendom,* vol. 2, p. 90-91, 179-80.

This style of mass evangelism is sometimes called "Billy Graham Evangelism," because of the most famous modern practitioner of the technique. It dates back to the 19th-century practices of the heretical American evangelist, Charles Finney.[20]

The one-on-one form of decisionalism has been greatly popularized by Campus Crusade's *Four Spiritual Laws*, and other programs of lay evangelism, such as *Evangelism Explosion*. If these techniques were restricted to fringe sects of free-will baptists, our criticisms would be quite limited. Yet, it is a sad commentary on the state of modern American religion, that these sorts of "gospel presentations" are pervasive in "evangelical" circles. These practices of evangelism are even tolerated and approved within "reformed" denominations.

1. These techniques betray an erroneous view of the human will. The practitioners of these methods inevitably give the impression (and sometimes openly state) that the sinner's will is determinative in salvation – in spite of the biblical declaration that election "is not of him that willeth, nor of him that runneth, but of God that showeth mercy" (Rom. 9:16).

The heresy of free will is implicit within the language commonly employed by evangelicals when they exhort men to "*accept* Christ as Saviour." This expression is not found any place in scripture; it communicates a false notion of *the sinner's sovereignty* in conversion, and it also helps to confound *historic* faith with *saving* faith. Given the sinful state of mankind, the pertinent question is not whether we "accept Christ," but whether God accepts us.

Evangelicals will speak of the guilt and effects of sin, thereby asserting that man was damaged at the fall of Adam. Yet, much

---

20. Michael Horton makes a passing reference to Finney as he discusses the popularization of Pelagian evangelism. In a footnote he states: 'Charles Finney denied original sin, the substitutionary atonement, the necessity of supernatural grace in the new birth, and argued that the doctrine "of justification by an imputed righteousness is another gospel."' See Horton's essay, "What Still Keeps Us Apart?" in John Armstrong, ed., *Roman Catholicism: Evangelicals Analyze What Divides and Unites Us* (Chicago: Moody Press, 1994), pp. 262-64, p. 266 (note 13).

like Rome, contemporary evangelicals deny the *inability* of fallen mankind, because they elevate the human will as the determinative factor in regeneration.

The heresy of free will has appeared many times in church history. When Pelagius espoused free will in the fourth century, he was opposed by Augustine. At the time of the Protestant Reformation, the Reformers vigorously opposed the advocates of free will.[21] In the 17th century, the Synod of Dordt recognized the association between Pelagianism and the tenets of Arminianism; the Synod condemned the Arminians for bringing "again out of hell the Pelagian error" of free will.[22]

Based upon the doctrine of free will, the evangelistic techniques of decisionalism were introduced by the 19th century American preacher, Charles Finney. Through Finney's influence, "evangelicalism underwent a major change in meaning. His Pelagianism subverted the Reformation's understanding of grace precisely because it denied the Reformation's view of man."[23]

---

21. It is worth noting that three of the major reformers wrote book-length treatises against free will. In *The Bondage of the Will* (1525), Luther contended against the free-will teaching of Erasmus; Calvin wrote a treatise *Concerning the Eternal Predestination of God* (1552) against the free will doctrine of Pighius; Knox denies free will in his *Answer to a Great Number of Blasphemous Cavillations Written by an Anabaptist, and Adversary to God's Eternal Predestination* (1560). This point of unity among the reformers demonstrates just how far modern evangelicals have departed from the doctrines of the Protestant Reformation.

22. Canons of the Synod of Dordt, 2nd Head, rejection 3. Cf. 1st Head, "Of Divine Predestination," rejection 4; 2nd Head, "Of the Death of Christ, and the Redemption of Men Thereby," rejection 6; 3rd and 4th Heads, "Of the Corruption of Man, His Conversion to God, and the Manner Thereof," article 2, article 10, rejection 7, rejection 9; 5th Head, "Of the Perseverance of the Saints," rejection 2.

23. Gerstner, John H. "The Theological Boundaries of Evangelical Faith," in *The Evangelicals: What They Believe, Who They Are, Where They Are Changing.* Edited by David F. Wells and John D. Woodbridge. (Nashville: Abingdon, 1975), p. 27.

Gerstner adds: "The price which has had to be paid is a diminished doctrine of grace. Although contemporary evangelists have recoiled from some

Anyone who truly believes in free will does not understand the fallen condition of mankind, and thus does not affirm the true nature of God's grace in salvation. God sovereignly draws his elect to Christ, as Jesus declares, "All that the Father giveth me shall come to me" (John 6:37). Because of the native inability of mankind, "No man can come to me, except the Father draw him" (John 6:44). The believing response of some hearers to the preaching of the gospel flows strictly from God's sovereign grace. "For who maketh thee to differ from another? and what hast thou that thou didst not receive?" (1 Cor. 4:7). "As many as were ordained to eternal life believed" (Acts 13:48). It must be sovereign grace, or it is not really grace at all. Evangelicals effectively deny the grace of God in salvation, inasmuch as they appeal to the sinner's will as determinative in salvation.

We know that decisionalists often decry sovereign grace, claiming it destroys efforts at evangelism. Historically, this is simply not the case. The Protestant Reformation was, in essence, a vast evangelistic effort, with a heavy emphasis on preaching. The reformers realized, however, that "without God's gracious interposition the preaching of the gospel will always be fruitless. God's sovereignty undergirds evangelism; it does not undermine it."[24]

2. The exercise of the sinner's will – making a decision – is equated with faith. The "decision" is viewed as the means to regeneration; "faith" is said to precede or produce regeneration and forgiveness of sins. Faith is seen as the cause of regeneration, not

---

of Finney's distortions, the evangel is still presented as being of divine origin but it is seen as needing human cooperation for its realization. The initiative of God in disposing man to receive the gospel is not only seen as unnecessary but some view it as pernicious since the freedom of man is thereby violated. The dilemma of relating man's moral inability to his ethical responsibility is not new to this generation of evangelicals, nor are some of the solutions that have emerged. But it is clear that the view common to the Protestant Reformers, which was held with remarkable unanimity, has undergone serious modifications" (p. 28).

24. Gerstner, John H. "The Theological Boundaries of Evangelical Faith," p. 28.

the fruit of it: hence, our description of this doctrine as *decisional regeneration.* Indeed, in this scheme of things, "faith" practically becomes the *ground of justification,* since converts are told to rest their assurance upon their decision for Christ. Thus, when evangelicals claim to believe in justification by faith alone, they often mean something radically different than the historic Protestant doctrine.[25]

3. The nature of conversions is rarely examined. Many persons confuse mental assent with faith; *temporary faith* is not distinguished from *saving faith.* One result is that many who make a profession of faith later fall away, and they are then categorized as "carnal Christians."[26]

At root, the scriptural doctrine of saving faith is almost completely absent among modern evangelicals. It has been replaced by spurious forms of faith, what Reformation Protestants would have called *historic faith* and *temporary faith.*

Due to the techniques of decisionalism, spurious professions should be expected. The practitioners of these evangelistic methods spend so much time preparing the mood of the audience, telling anecdotes, and pressing for decisions, that Christ is rarely preached in the fulness necessary for hearers to make an intelligent profession of faith. The hearers are exhorted to place their "faith" in an unknown Saviour – a person whom they know too little about to rest upon for salvation.

---

25. Part of the confusion over terminology is caused by a belief in universal atonement. Since modern evangelicals generally believe that Christ has died and paid the price for all the sins of every man (both elect and reprobate), the substitutionary death of Christ cannot be the determinative basis of one's standing before God. Therefore, the sinner's decision, in accepting Christ, is made the determining factor in the application of redemption. In a very real sense, then, the sinner's decision is the effective cause of salvation.

26. For a refutation of the "carnal Christian" theory, see Ernest C. Reisinger, *What Should We Think of the Carnal Christian?* (Edinburgh: Banner of Truth, 1978).

By contrast, Christ must be preached and known "as he is offered in the gospel:"[27] that is, in his offices of prophet, priest and king. The confusion in respect to the person of Christ has reached such alarming proportions, that a debate has erupted among evangelicals over "the lordship controversy." The puritan preacher Thomas Manton summarizes the root problem: "Many would admit Christ to be their advocate to plead for them, but not their king to rule over them."[28]

As we noted earlier, genuine faith not only possesses a right understanding of Christ's person; it is joined with other saving graces which will never be found in these "carnal Christians" who populate the pews of modern evangelicalism. In the Bible, justification precedes sanctification, and the two concepts cannot be divorced, as though the one will exist to the exclusion of the other.[29]

4. Many contemporary evangelicals confound justification with regeneration; like Rome, they confuse the legal (external) nature of justification with the inward work of God in renewing the sinner. In the past two decades, there has been an enormous emphasis on the necessity of being "born again."[30] This focus has led to an over-emphasis on the *experiential* aspects of salvation, to the virtual exclusion of the forensic nature of justification. The result is that the doctrine of justification has been eclipsed by a doctrine

---

27. Westminster Shorter Catechism #86; see also, "Saving Faith," pp. 6-8 above.

28. *A Body of Divinity* (1692; rpt. Edinburgh: Banner of Truth, 1992), p. 188. He adds, "Say not, as those Jews, 'We have no king but Caesar,' no king but our lusts.... Submit to Christ willingly. All the devils in hell submit to Christ; but it is against their will; they are his slaves, not his subjects. Many would have Christ their saviour, but not their prince; such as will not have Christ to be their king to rule over them, shall never have his blood to save them" (p. 191).

29. See note 1 above.

30. This exhortation could be useful, if evangelicals adhered to the scriptural doctrine of regeneration as the sovereign work of God's Spirit. Instead, most evangelicals see the new birth as the result of the sinner exercising his will.

of "letting Jesus into your heart." That is, the external basis of justification (by Christ's imputed righteousness) has been replaced by a quest for the inward experience of being "born again."[31]

It is significant to note that the older Protestant doctrinal formulations placed the discussion of regeneration solidly within the context of the broader scope of redemption. For example, the Westminster Confession has no separate chapter on regeneration; instead, regeneration is covered under the subject of effectual calling, and then only by way of a description.[32] Later, as the standards move to the subject of sanctification, further reference is made to regeneration: "They who are effectually called and regenerated, having a new heart and a new spirit created in them, are further sanctified really and personally, through the virtue of Christ's death and resurrection, by his word and Spirit dwelling in them...."[33] By setting forth regeneration in relation to effectual calling and sanctification, the Westminster Standards avoid an imbalanced portrayal of the doctrine.

Of course, most contemporary evangelicals do not embrace the biblical doctrine of regeneration as the sovereign work of God. Therefore, neither the biblical doctrine of regeneration, nor the biblical doctrine of justification have much currency in contem-

---

31. John Armstrong relates an interesting incident which illustrates this point. 'I will never forget the first time I led a young man into a decision, not realizing then that such evangelistic methodology is more Roman Catholic than genuinely evangelical, only to ask him the so-called follow-up question, "Where is Christ right now?" He answered happily, "I have received Him into my heart in prayer with you, just as I receive Him into my heart every time I take the Mass."' (Armstrong, "The Evangelical Moment?" Chapter 13 of *Roman Catholicism: Evangelicals Analyze What Divides and Unites Us*, pp. 306-07). Stating his uneasiness with modern evangelism, Armstrong expresses many legitimate criticisms. Yet he fails to follow through with the implications of his observations. After all, if both Rome and evangelicals have corrupted the gospel, why should either group be regarded as a true Christian church? See chapter 4 below for a discussion of such issues.

32. Confession, 10:1; Larger Catechism #67; Shorter Catechism #31.

33. Confession, 13:1.

porary evangelical circles. There is quite a contrast between reformation preaching and modern preaching. Reformed preachers sought to impress hearers with their need for deliverance from the guilt of sin; modern preachers try to lure converts with the benefits they will experience by making a decision for Christ. The former preaching was God-centered and objective in nature; modern preaching is man-centered and subjective in focus.

From the foregoing discussion, it should be clear that contemporary evangelicals have exchanged the biblical gospel for another gospel. They have subverted the grace of the gospel by asserting human ability (free will) to obtain salvation. They have confounded justification and regeneration; they have sought regeneration by the performance of religious rituals (the alter call, the sinner's prayer).

Summary

Thus we see that both contemporary evangelicals and Roman Catholics subvert the biblical way of salvation. Both oppose the scriptural doctrine of redemption, as espoused by the Protestant Reformers. The solemn words of the apostle apply to both evangelicals and Roman Catholics together: "But though we, or an angel from heaven, preach any other gospel unto you than that which we have preached unto you, let him be accursed" (Gal. 1:8).

Chapter 3

The Way of Worship

In the first chapter, we examined the biblical doctrine of redemption, and we saw that both Roman Catholics and evangelicals have departed from the scriptural understanding of the Protestant Reformation. In this chapter we will examine scriptural principles of worship, and use them to measure the worship practices of both Rome and present-day evangelicalism.

Biblical Teaching on Worship

It was a glorious day in ancient Israel. The tabernacle had recently been built according to the divine blueprint given to Moses by the Lord (Ex. 25:8-9). Aaron and his sons were consecrated to their priestly vocation, and they offered the prescribed sacrifices unto God (Lev. 8-9). The "glory of the Lord appeared unto all the people." Fire came out from the Lord and lit the offering on the altar, consuming the sacrifice, "which when all the people saw, they shouted, and fell on their faces" (Lev. 9:23-24). We can only imagine the mixture of awe, wonder, and joy which the people experienced on this holy and festive occasion.

Moments later, the scene changed dramatically, as a terrible judgment fell upon Nadab and Abihu. In the midst of their activities, "there went out fire from the Lord, and devoured them, and they died before the Lord" (Lev. 10:2).

What had they done, to provoke the anger of the Lord? The biblical narrative tells us simply that they "offered strange fire before the Lord, which he commanded them not" (Lev. 10:1).

Nadab and Abihu had not done something which was expressly forbidden. No, they merely added a bit of "strange fire" which the Lord had not commanded. The judgment which came upon them stands as a perpetual testimony against those who presume to worship God by means which lack divine warrant. It is a solemn warning: "the LORD spake, saying, I will be sanctified in them that come nigh me, and before all the people I will be glorified" (Lev. 10:3).

God's displeasure with synthetic worship is expressed throughout scripture. In order to gain a better understanding of scriptural principles of worship, we will make a further examination of precepts and examples from the Bible.

Biblical Precepts

In the book of Deuteronomy, Moses exhorts the children of Israel to keep the law of God. In chapter 12, he reviews scriptural precepts pertaining to worship.

The LORD forbids his people to imitate pagan ways of worship; the Israelites were commanded to eradicate the remnants of corrupt worship from their midst. They were commanded to destroy "all the *places*" wherein the heathen served their gods. They were instructed to purge the land of all the *implements* associated with false worship: "Ye shall overthrow their altars, and break their pillars, and burn their groves with fire; and ye shall hew down the graven images of their gods." Even the *terminology* of corrupt worship was to be erased: "Destroy the names of them out of that place" (Deut. 12:2-3).

To the modern mind, this may sound strangely intolerant. But the LORD warned his people against the danger of imitating the worship practices of the pagans: "Ye shall not do so unto the LORD your God." The chapter concludes with a further warning against imitating heathen worship. "Take heed to thyself that thou be not snared by following them, after that they be destroyed from before thee; and that thou inquire not after their gods, saying, How did these nations serve their gods? even so will I do likewise. Thou shalt not do so unto the LORD thy God.... What thing soever I command you, observe to do it: thou shalt not add thereto, nor diminish from it" (Deut. 12:30-32; cf. 4:2).

The sufficiency and authority of scripture are brought to bear upon the content of our worship. This is the meaning of the scriptural law of worship: all forms of worship must have express scriptural warrant, if they are to be admitted as legitimate means of worship.[1] The biblical pattern of worship needs no supplements of human devising; indeed, such man-made innovations are a snare – the very seed of idolatry.

When we consider the fallen nature of mankind, we see why the biblical precepts of worship are necessary. Since the fall of Adam, the nature of man has been thoroughly corrupt. This inherent corruption drives men away from God: "There is none that understandeth, there is none that seeketh after God" (Rom. 3:11). Thus, the native tendency of mankind is to pollute the worship of God, exchanging the truth of God for a lie, worshipping and serving created things rather than the Creator (Rom. 1:25).

Just as men are incapable of forging a method for their own salvation, so they are incapable of devising proper means to worship and serve God. Therefore, the only proper way to worship God is through the means established by the LORD himself.

Worship in the Wilderness

During the wilderness wanderings, the Israelites had to be schooled in proper principles of worship. Their native tendency toward corrupt worship was shown early, while they waited for Moses to return from Mt. Sinai. Growing restless, Aaron and the people constructed a golden calf to serve as a visible symbol of deity.

Virtually all expositors decry the action of the Israelites as idolatry. What is often overlooked, however, is the manner in which the Israelites justified their action. They did not view the calf as a newly-created deity; rather, they made the calf as a testimony of

1. "The acceptable way of worshipping the true God is instituted by himself, and so limited by his own revealed will, that he may not be worshipped according to the imaginations and devices of men, or the suggestions of Satan, under any visible representation, or any other way not prescribed in holy scripture" (Westminster Confession, 21:1).

their divine deliverance from Egypt. The calf-image evoked a sense of the strength displayed in their deliverance. "These be thy gods, O Israel, which brought thee up out of the land of Egypt. And when Aaron saw it, he built an altar before it; and Aaron made proclamation, and said, Tomorrow is a feast to the LORD" (Ex. 32:4-5).

In other words, the Israelites did not claim to worship new deities – that would be blatant idolatry. No, they intended the calf to serve as a symbol of deity; and Aaron seeks to honor the sacred name of the LORD through this monstrous invention.[2]

Now, when Moses returned, he did not regard this matter lightly. He did not employ the tactic which Papists have used for centuries (and which evangelical churchmen presently endorse), simply cautioning the Israelites not to worship false gods, noting that the image itself was not a deity, and then allowing the image to remain strictly as a symbol. Moses "took the calf which they had made, and burnt it in the fire, and ground it to powder, and strawed it upon the water, and made the children of Israel drink of it. And Moses said unto Aaron, What did this people unto thee, that thou hast brought so great a sin upon them?" (Ex. 32:20-21).

---

2. Even the Anglican author, J. I. Packer, explains this incident as an attempt by Aaron to worship the LORD (not other gods) – an attempt using unlawful means. "Aaron made a golden calf (that is, a bull-image). It was meant as a visible symbol of Jehovah, the mighty God who brought Israel out of Egypt. No doubt the image was thought to honor Him, as being a fitting symbol of His great strength. But it is not hard to see that such a symbol in fact insults Him: for what idea of His moral character, His righteousness, goodness, and patience, could one gather from looking at a statue of Him as a bull? Thus Aaron's image hid Jehovah's glory. In a similar way, the pathos of the crucifix obscures the glory of Christ, for it hides the fact of His deity, His victory on the cross, and His present kingdom. It displays His human weakness, but it conceals His divine strength; it depicts the reality of His pain, but keeps out of our sight the reality of His joy and His power. In both cases, the symbol is unworthy most of all because of what it fails to display. And so are all other visible representations of Deity." *Knowing God* (Downers Grove: InterVarsity Press, 1973), pp. 40-41.

This sin had transpired while Moses was receiving the ten commandments on the mountain. And the decalogue forbids not only the worship of false Gods, but it also condemns the worship of the true God by unsanctioned methods.

The Scriptural Law of Worship

The first commandment declares, "Thou shalt have no other gods before me" (Ex. 20:3). It is plain that the LORD God is the only proper recipient of worship.

The second commandment continues the focus on worship by telling us *how God is to be worshipped.* It does so in a negative sense, by forbidding us to worship God with human inventions. "Thou shalt not make unto thee any graven image" (Ex. 20:4).

A graven image is not merely a statue of a false deity. If that were the case, the second commandment would be redundant of the first. Instead, the second commandment plainly forbids making or revering physical or artistic representations of the true God.

When the LORD revealed himself to the Israelites, he did so by means of his word – not by physical images to be imitated or embellished. Therefore, he warned them: "Take ye therefore good heed unto yourselves; for ye saw no manner of similitude on the day that the LORD spake unto you in Horeb out of the midst of the fire: lest ye corrupt yourselves, and make you a graven image, the similitude of any figure," etc. (Deut. 4:15-16).[3]

The apostle Paul instructed the Athenians, "We ought not to think that the Godhead is like unto gold, or silver, or stone, graven

---

3. Readers should note that Roman Catholics and Lutherans divide the ten commandments differently than ordinary Protestants. Papists and Lutherans combine the first two commandments into one, thus subsuming the second command as a mere appendix to the first. They divide the tenth commandment into two commands prohibiting different kinds of covetousness. Thus, they still maintain ten in number, but the effects on their doctrine of worship is devastating.

In practice, many modern Protestants have unwittingly adopted this same viewpoint. The second commandment is expounded as a mere expansion of the first, and restricted in application only to false deities and open homby art and man's device" (Acts 17:29). Any attempt to represent God by human devices is an insult to the LORD. His pronouncement is clear: "I am the LORD: that is my name: and my glory will I not give to another, neither my praise to graven images" (Isa. 42:8).

The prohibition expressed in the second commandment reaches beyond what we might call an image, in the strictest sense of the term. In its broader scope, this commandment really forbids the use of all man-made devices in worship. It directs us to a basic concept: that the only acceptable way of worshipping God is to render homage to him according to the instructions given in his word. Any deviation from his word by adopting humanly-devised forms of worship is, *de facto*, a violation of the scriptural law of worship.

In other words, all religious ceremonies and institutions must have clear scriptural warrant, if they are to be admitted as valid expressions of worship. This concept has sometimes been called the regulative principle of worship. It is merely an application of the *sola scriptura* rule of Protestant theology.

Temple Worship

The designation of a central place of worship did not occur until the Israelites conquered and settled the land of Canaan. A central site for public worship had been anticipated since the time of Moses (Deut. 12:11; cf. 12:5, 14); but it did not reach fulfillment until the reign of David. During David's rule, the ark of the covenant was moved to Jerusalem, thereby establishing the city as the center for the sacrificial ordinances of the Levitical priesthood. Even so, the entire program of worship, from the tabernacle to the temple, was directed by divine revelation.

Tabernacle worship was structured according to the divine blueprint. The Israelites were instructed: "Let them make me a sanc-

---

age to images. As a result, they admit images into churches, ostensibly for didactic purposes. This modern interpretation is contrary to the Protestant confessions of the Reformation. See Heidelberg Catechism #96-98, Westminster Confession, 21:2-3; Westminster Larger Catechism, #107-109.

tuary; that I may dwell among them. According to all that I shew thee, after the pattern of all the instruments thereof, even so shall ye make it." Descriptions of the tabernacle furnishings reiterated that all things had to be made according to the God-given pattern (Ex. 25:8-9; cf. 25:40; 27:8; Num. 8:4; Acts 7:44; Heb. 8:5).

Later, David provided Solomon with the plan for constructing the temple: "David gave to Solomon his son the pattern of the porch, and of the houses thereof ... and the pattern of all that he had by the spirit.... also for the courses of the priests and the Levites.... All this, said David, the LORD made me understand in writing by his hand upon me, even all the works of this pattern" (1 Chron. 28:11-13, 19). Nothing was left for improvising; everything was ordered by the divine pattern for worship.

Solomon built the temple according to the heavenly blueprints left by David, and Jerusalem remained the seat of public worship for the entire kingdom of Israel.

After the death of Solomon, the kingdom became divided and the people slid into corruption and apostasy. The northern tribes swiftly embraced false worship, and never recovered from their apostasy. Within the kingdom of Judah, there were several seasons of reformation, amidst other waves of idolatry. The key to understanding the history of the Israelites it to note the critical connection between the worship of the people, and God's dealings with them in relation to their worship.

The Apostasy of the Northern Kingdom

When the northern tribes seceded, Jeroboam took a pragmatic approach to worship in the northern kingdom, devising a "local" program of worship suited to his own purposes (1 Kings 12:28-33). Jeroboam's actions were wholly revolutionary. He established a new center for worship, new means for worship, and a new priesthood. It was not so much that Jeroboam encouraged his people to worship other deities, but that he devised new methods which displaced the biblical means of worship; Jeroboam's offense was akin to Aaron's sin in making the original golden calf.

Subsequent kings in the north, such as Ahab, blatantly embraced the worship of Baal. Later, when Jehu ruled the northern kingdom, he exterminated the house of Ahab, and repudiated the Baalism of his predecessors. Yet for all his zeal, Jehu retained the "sins of Jeroboam, which made Israel to sin" (2 Kings 10:29-31).

The reign of Jehu indicates that the guilt of Israel came not merely from idolatry, in the narrow sense of the term: that is, the worship of false deities. Jehu eradicated the worship of other deities and claimed to worship the Lord, but he clung to the unhallowed *methods* of worship instituted by Jeroboam. Thus, Israel was charged with corrupt worship for attempting to worship the true God, the Lord, with unsanctioned means.

The comparison here between Jeroboam and Jehu again illustrates that Jeroboam's original crime was in establishing alternative forms of worship from those enjoined in the Mosaic law. Jeroboam's initial action took Israel to the slippery slope of corrupt worship. From there, the nation frequently degenerated into further idolatry by worshipping false gods as well. Therefore, let it be noted that the first step on the path of idolatry is taken when men presume to worship the Lord through means and measures not ordained in the word of God.

The kings of northern Israel were idolaters; the apostasy of the nation was thorough; and so the Lord destroyed the northern kingdom. A chilling account is provided in 2 Kings 17:4ff., with a summary judgment in verses 20-24 of that same chapter.

The 17th chapter of 2 Kings also explains the origin of the mongrel religion of the Samaritans. After the Assyrians conquered the northern kingdom of Israel, the Assyrian king deported the Israelites; he then used the land of Israel as a relocation center for Babylonians and other displaced persons (2 Kings 17:24-41). These heathen refugees "feared not the Lord: therefore the Lord sent lions among them, which slew some of them" (2 Kings 17:25).

Alarmed by this development, the king of Assyria sent back an Israelite priest to instruct the people how to serve the Lord. The people then professed to worship the Lord God, but they attempted to render service to the LORD by resorting to their customary idolatry, employing their own devices and priesthood. "So they feared the LORD, and made unto themselves of the lowest of them priests of the high places, which sacrificed for them in the houses of the high places. They feared the LORD, and served their own gods, after the manner of the nations whom they carried away from thence.... So these nations feared the LORD, and served their graven images, both their children, and their children's children: as did their fathers, so do they unto this day" (2 Kings 17:32-33, 41).

The technical term for such a religious admixture is *syncretism.* For centuries it has been the *modus operandi* of Roman Catholicism. Sadly this Samaritan approach to worship is only too prominent among professing Protestants and in the church growth movement among contemporary "evangelicals." The trends in popular culture and the deviant worship of the pluralistic masses are adopted as a way to make worship "relevant" and appealing to modern society.

The Kingdom of Judah

After the separation of the northern tribes, the kingdom of Judah often embraced corrupt worship, beginning with the reign of Rehoboam: "Judah did evil in the sight of the LORD, and they provoked him to jealousy with their sins which they had committed, above all that their fathers had done. For they also built them high places, and images, and groves, on every high hill, and under every green tree. And there were also sodomites in the land: and they did according to all the abominations of the nations which the LORD cast out before the children of Israel" (1 Kings 14:22-24).[4]

When Asa became king in Judah, he instituted reform. In the scriptural account of his reign, he is commended for removing corrupt worship. "Asa did that which was good and right in the

---

4. Today, many Roman Catholics and evangelicals decry the sins of abortion and homosexuality as manifestations of our nation's corruptions (which they are); but these contemporary moralists are generally silent about the heinous sin of corrupt worship.

eyes of the LORD his God: for he took away the altars of the strange gods, and the high places, and brake down the images, and cut down the groves: and commanded Judah to seek the LORD God of their fathers, and to do the law and the commandment. Also he took away out of all the cities of Judah the high places and the images: and the kingdom was quiet before him" (2 Chron. 15:2-5; cf. 1 Kings 15:12-19).

Among the later kings there were both good and evil rulers. What is striking about the biblical narratives is that kings are consistently measured by their approach to worship. Those rulers who made an effort to restore biblical worship are commended; those kings who resorted to idolatry (or tolerated corrupt worship) are criticized.

During the reign of godly King Jehoshaphat, the people manifested an attachment to corrupt worship, in spite of efforts by the king to reform the land. "The people had not prepared their hearts unto the God of their fathers." Many resorted to sites of corrupt worship, "for the people offered and burnt incense in the high places," and these high places were not taken away (2 Chron. 20:33; 1 Kings 22:43; 2 Chron. 20:33).

Corrupt worship reveals a serious problem of the heart. In conducting unsanctioned worship, the people showed that their hearts were not right with God, regardless of what their professed motives might have been.

In subsequent generations, the kingdom of Judah degenerated into further idolatry and Baal worship. "They left the house of the LORD of their fathers, and served groves and idols: and wrath came upon Judah and Jerusalem for this their trespass" (2 Chron. 24:18).

Could anything be clearer? The LORD detests corrupt worship and he punishes this sin.

Hezekiah was a good king, and he issued a call for national repentance; he also established a program of reform (2 Kings 18:5-6; 2 Chron. 30).

The passover was restored. Moreover, the people "arose and took away the altars that were in Jerusalem, and all the altars for incense took they away, and cast them into the brook Kidron ... all Israel that were present went out to the cities of Judah, and brake the images in pieces, and cut down the groves, and threw down the high places and the altars out of all Judah and Benjamin, in Ephraim also and Manasseh, until they had utterly destroyed them all" (2 Chron. 30:14; 31:1).

Under Hezekiah's leadership, we see two aspects of reform united: the positive work of restoring the biblical pattern of worship, and the negative work of removing the elements of unscriptural worship. Both aspects are essential components of thorough reform.

As a negative facet of reform, Hezekiah "brake the images, and cut down the groves, and brake in pieces the brasen serpent that Moses had made: for unto those days the children of Israel did burn incense to it: and he called it Nehushtan [*a piece of brass*]" (2 Chron. 18:4).

The destruction of the brasen serpent is an extremely important event, for it demonstrates the far-reaching scope of genuine reform. The brasen serpent was originally made at the command of God. It had not, however, been designated as an implement for use in the ordinary worship of the LORD. Therefore, because the brasen serpent had been superstitiously abused, it was necessary to destroy it.

Contemporary readers may find it difficult to comprehend this deed. It is easier to discern why Hezekiah led the people to destroy the high places, images, and groves dedicated to unsanctioned worship. But, truly, the brasen serpent was a hallowed symbol of God's former deliverance of the Israelites. Why destroy it? Why not simply caution the people against the abuse of a traditional symbol?

Hezekiah was wiser than both Papists and our modern evangelical churchmen, who would, no doubt, follow a more "moderate" course. The king realized that the serpent had become a snare; it fostered superstition. And Hezekiah knew that this superstition – this corruption of worship – was sufficient to provoke the wrath of God. Far better to dispense with a sacred relic, than leave it as a temptation for present and future generations.

As noted, the brasen serpent was included in no part of the ordinary worship of God. By comparison, the passover was an integral part of the stated worship of God; therefore the passover was renewed and restored. But since the serpent had no sanctioned role in the stated worship of God, it was better to remove it altogether.

After Hezekiah's rule the nation again drifted into apostasy. The last reforming king was Josiah.[5] In addition to purging the kingdom of corrupt worship, the young king directed repairs of the house of the LORD (2 Chron. 34-35; 2 Kings 22). After Josiah's death, the kingdom of Judah passed again into apostasy. The nation then fell to the Babylonians, and the Jewish people were carried away into exile.

Eventually, the Jews were permitted to return to their homeland and commence rebuilding the temple in Jerusalem. They were careful to restore the temple and its services according to the scriptural pattern (Ezra 3:10). When the construction was complete, "they set the priests in their divisions, and the Levites in their courses, for the service of God, which is at Jerusalem; as it is written in the book of Moses" (Ezra 6:18). Moreover, the passover was restored (Ezra 3:10; 6:18, 20-22).

---

5. He purged "Judah and Jerusalem from the high places, and the groves, and the carved images, and the molten images. And they brake down the altars of Baalim in his presence; and the images, that were on high above them, he cut down; and the groves, and the carved images, and the molten images, he brake in pieces, and made dust of them, and strewed it upon the graves of them that had sacrificed unto them. And he burnt the bones of the priests upon their altars, and cleansed Judah and Jerusalem. And so did he in the cities of Manasseh, and Ephraim, and Simeon, even unto Naphtali, with their mattocks round about. And when he had broken down the altars and the groves, and had beaten the graven images into powder, and cut down all the idols throughout all the land of Israel, he returned to Jerusalem" (2 Chron. 34:3-7; cf. 2 Kings 23:4-14, 24).

Christ's Teaching on Worship

Christ reinforces the Old Testament commandments which restrict the object of worship to the LORD God alone. When assaulted by the suggestion to worship Satan, Jesus replied, "Get thee hence, Satan: for it is written, Thou shalt worship the Lord thy God, and him only shalt thou serve" (Matt. 4:10).

The 15th chapter of Matthew records a different kind of conflict between Christ and corrupt worship – the confrontation between Christ and Jewish religious leaders of his day. In considering this passage, we should recall that the scribes and the Pharisees were not heathen idolaters. They did not worship Baal, nor did they bow before the state god, Caesar. They did not make graven images, adhering to the strict letter of the law. They had a high regard for the temple in Jerusalem, which they knew to be the prescribed place for the public ordinances. But was their religion scriptural?

No. The scribes and Pharisees held to the traditions of their fathers so zealously, that their traditional practices had, in many respects superceded the precepts of the Old Testament (Matt. 15:2). Hence, the apostle Paul later refers to this traditionalism as "the Jews' religion," indicating that apostate Judaism is not the religion of the Bible (Gal. 1:13-14).

A conflict was created, because these Jews sought to supplement the biblical precepts with practices of their own devising. Jesus rebukes them for substituting man-made duties in the place of God-given responsibilities. "Why do ye also transgress the commandment of God by your tradition?" (Matt. 15:3).

The Saviour then exposes the method of subterfuge the Pharisees had invented in order to cover their negligence. They had cloaked corrupt practices by claiming a high regard for the temple, the focal point of public worship. Yet, their argument was merely a pretence for neglecting family duties prescribed in the law.

As a result, the divine verdict was against them: "This people draweth nigh unto me with their mouth, and honoureth me with their lips; but their heart is far from me. But in vain do they worship me, teaching for doctrines the commandments of men" (Matt. 15:8-9; cf. Isa. 29:13).

Here Christ draws a connection between the religious service performed by these men, and the worship which they offer. Their worship was eclipsed by the spurious religious traditions which they annexed to it.

This rebuke clearly condemns the notion that mankind (or the church as an institution) has the right to institute new modes of worship and religious service. If men assert the right to invent new forms of religious piety, they are usurping the authority which belongs to God alone. Christ is the King of the church, the only lawgiver.

The Pharisees paid lip service to God. We know they made long prayers, fasted twice a week, and arranged financial bequests to the temple. As formalists, they were exceedingly concerned about outward conformity to man-made regulations. At first, we might not link their practices to "public worship," since many of these activities were conducted outside the temple and synagogue services. Yet, their traditional observances are accounted by Christ a measure of their worship. And their worship is declared to be vain.

The Essence of True Worship

Christ describes the essence of true worship during his conversation with the woman at the well (John 4:5-26). During the conversation, the woman propounds to Jesus the preeminent religious controversy which existed between the Jews and the Samaritans.

Specifically, the dispute was over where to worship. Now, it is true that God had prescribed Jerusalem as the place for public ordinances – although that would soon change. Outwardly, as regards the place for public ordinances, the Jews were right. God had prescribed a pattern of worship which was focused upon Jerusalem. This divine pattern was designed as a witness for all mankind, regarding the right way of salvation. "Salvation is of the

Jews" (John 4:22), for "unto them were committed the oracles of God" (Rom. 3:22). In this sense, the Jews worshipped what they knew: that is, they adhered to the knowledge of the law as it pertained to the place for divine ordinances. (Herein we are again directed to the importance of revealed religion, as given in the law.) The Samaritans had abandoned the law, and forged their own mongrel religion (2 Kings 17).

In another manner, Jesus reiterates the importance of God's appointment in religion. A great change was about to occur, respecting the outward ordinances of worship. At whose direction? Not by man's appointment, but by the appointment of God. He alone is the lawgiver. None may tamper with the pattern which he has established; yet it is his divine prerogative to make alterations in conformity with his purposes.

Jesus next summarizes the essence of true worship, which includes the inseparable union of both piety and knowledge. True worshippers shall worship God "in spirit and in the truth." The worship of true worshippers is characterized in this manner, as an outworking of God's saving grace. God's sovereignty in salvation extends not only to the manner in which the elect are saved, but also to the purposes for which they are redeemed. One essential design in the salvation of the elect is that they shall worship in spirit and truth: "for the Father seeketh such to worship him" (John 4:23).

The language is repeated in imperative form. It is language similar to other imperatives in the teaching of Christ, such as the statement recorded in the previous chapter of John's gospel: "Ye *must* be born again." The true worshippers "*shall* worship the Father in spirit and in truth.... they that worship him *must* worship him in spirit and in truth" (John 3:7; 4:23-24).

True worship must be "in spirit." It involves the inner man, demanding sincerity and love. Worship includes more than the mere outward forms of devotion. Many times God has pronounced a curse against persons wedded to empty forms of religion. The unbelieving Jews had hearts far from the LORD, even though they were in the right place for external ordinances. True worship must flow from hearts of sincerity and love toward God our Saviour.

Likewise, genuine worship must be "in truth." That is, our worship must be in conformity to God's written revelation. There is, indeed, an outward measure for our worship. In the present day, it is common to hear comments that the "heart" is all that matters: a mistaken concept that sincerity of motive and fervent emotion are the substance of genuine worship. But Christ does not confine the essence of worship to worship in spirit; he adds the measure of truth. Acceptable worship is more than the gushy effervescence of a fervent heart. Without truth, such fervor is an offense before God; it is zeal, "but not according to knowledge"[6] (Rom. 10:2).

Christ's statements imply a solemn warning. By his reference to "true worshippers" (John 4:23), we may perceive a distinction which sets them apart from other worshippers. In other words, there is a class of worshippers who are false in their worship. Therefore, we must examine our own worship carefully, that we may discern to which class we belong.

The New Era Following the Death of Christ

As Christ indicated to the woman at the well, a great change was occurring; it would render the dispute between Samaritans and Jews obsolete. When Christ died upon the cross, he exclaimed, "It is finished" (John 19:30), and the veil of the temple was torn in two "from the top to the bottom" (Matt. 27:51). This event marked the fulfillment of the Levitical ordinances of the Old Testament. Formerly, "the priests went always into the first tabernacle, accomplishing the service of God" (Heb. 9:6, 24; cf. Heb. 8:2). Now "Christ is not entered into the holy places made with hands which are the figures of the true; but into heaven itself, now to appear in

6. This defective view of worship may be linked to the tendency among evangelicals to define themselves subjectively (in terms of similar religious experiences), apart from objective commitments (in terms of biblical truth).

the presence of God for us." The earthly tabernacle (and temple) had always been a mere "example and shadow of heavenly things" (Heb. 8:5; 10:1; Col. 2:17). Now that the substance is manifest in Christ, the types and shadows give way to reality.

Through his priestly offering on the cross, Jesus "by himself purged our sins" and "sat down on the right hand of the Majesty on high" (Heb. 1:3). Having been declared "a priest for ever after the order of Melchisedec," Christ rendered the Levitical priesthood obsolete (Heb. 5:6).

This discussion is important on two counts: it shows the obsolescence of the older, ceremonial forms of worship along with the Levitical priesthood, and it indicates the end of sacrifice for sin.

With "the priesthood being changed" (Heb. 7:12), and the temple ceremonies having fulfilled their purpose, Jerusalem is no longer the fixed locale for the preeminent expressions of public worship. With the Old Testament ceremonies gone, what remains?

Apostolic Practice and Teaching

Although temple worship has reached its conclusion, several ordinary elements of worship continue. These are practices of piety which always had been found beyond the precincts of the temple – in private worship, family worship, and the synagogues – practices such as prayer, the reading of scripture, and biblical instruction.

We are told that the church "continued steadfastly in the apostles' doctrine and fellowship, and in breaking bread and prayers" (Acts 2:42). As Christ's commissioned messengers, the apostles arranged things according to divine directives. They had been ordered to "observe all things whatsoever" Christ commanded (Matt. 28:20). The church still was not permitted to worship and serve God according to human wisdom or man-made devices. Therefore, the apostles' doctrine was not something invented by the apostles; it was simply the doctrine of Christ – the doctrine of the holy scriptures.

Under the direction of the apostles, the reading and exposition of the scriptures were regular activities in the public assemblies of the church. These practices were ancient, "for Moses of old time hath in every city them that preach him, being read in the synagogues every sabbath day" (Acts 15:21; cf. 2 Cor. 3:15).

Since the apostles were Christ's appointed messengers, apostolic epistles were also read publicly as part of the canon of scripture. Paul commands, "I charge you by the Lord that this epistle be read unto all the holy brethren" (1 Thess. 5:27). "And when this epistle is read among you, cause that it be read also in the church of the Laodiceans; and that ye likewise read the epistle from Laodicea" (Col. 4:16).

Closely tied to the reading of the scriptures was the practice of expounding the word by public preaching and teaching. Jesus routinely expounded the word of God within assemblies for public worship: "Jesus went about all the cities and villages, teaching in their synagogues, and preaching the gospel of the kingdom" (Matt. 9:35). Thus it is not surprising to see the apostles adopting the same course: "And daily in the temple, and in every house, they ceased not to teach and preach Jesus Christ" (Acts 5:42). Later, Paul and Barnabas abode in Antioch, "teaching and preaching the word of the Lord, with many others also" (Acts 15:35). Before Paul departed from Troas, "upon the first day of the week, when the disciples came together to break bread, Paul preached unto them" (Acts 20:7).

Preaching was obviously a regular part of public worship. Hence the apostolic aspirations, "I am ready to preach the gospel to you that are at Rome also" (Rom. 1:15), and the apostolic admonitions: "Preach the word; be instant in season, out of season; reprove, rebuke, exhort with all longsuffering and doctrine" (2 Tim. 4:2).

Fellowship

The reference in Acts 2:42 to fellowship points to an important truth. Although temple worship has been discontinued, that does not mean that religious duties are now limited to private and family exercises. There yet remains a role for congregational worship and public ordinances. The public exercises of worship are no longer centered around a particular location (Jerusalem); nevertheless, corporate obligations are extensive among the people of God. For this reason, we find an apostolic admonition to provoke one another "unto love and to good works: not forsaking the assembling of ourselves together, as the manner of some is" (Heb. 10:24-25).

Wherever the gospel was received, gathered congregations were formed and organized (cf. Acts 14:21-23). It is in the context of the congregation assembled corporately that we find many expressions of public worship and service. Therefore we see why it was mentioned as an important factor that the early Christians continued steadfastly in apostolic fellowship. Corporate worship is the highest public expression of adoration rendered unto God.[7]

The Sacraments

Although the ceremonies of the temple have reached their fulfillment, the church is not left without any outward signs or seals of God's covenant. Rather, the Lord's Supper and baptism serve as a visible word to compliment the word preached.

The Lord's Supper was instituted by Jesus on the night before his crucifixion. It was a commanded ordinance; the language is plain: "Take, eat.... Drink ye...." "This do in remembrance of me" (Matt. 26:26; Luke 22:19-20; cf. Mark 14:22-23).

That these actions were meant to be an ongoing observance, is clear from both the words of the Saviour, and the apostolic commentary provided in 1 Cor. 11: 23-26: "For I have received of the Lord that which also I delivered unto you, that the Lord Jesus the same night in which he was betrayed took bread: and when he

---

7. A puritan writer, David Clarkson, explores this theme in a provocative sermon, "Public Worship to be Preferred Before Private," based upon Psalm 87:2: "The Lord loveth the gates of Zion more than all the dwellings of Jacob." See *The Practical Works of David Clarkson* (1865; rpt. Edinburgh: Banner of Truth, 1988), vol. 3, pp. 187-209.

had given thanks, he brake it, and said, Take, eat: this is my body, which is broken for you: this do in remembrance of me. After the same manner also he took the cup, when he had supped, saying, This cup is the new testament in my blood: this do ye, as oft as ye drink it, in remembrance of me. For as often as ye eat this bread, and drink this cup, ye do show the Lord's death till he come."

The divine warrant for baptism should be unquestioned, since it is embedded in the words of the Great Commission. "Go ye therefore, and teach all nations, baptizing them in the name of the Father, and of the Son, and of the Holy Ghost: teaching them to observe all things whatsoever I have commanded you: and, lo, I am with you always, even unto the end of the world. Amen." (Matt. 28:19-20). Numerous baptisms are recorded throughout the book of Acts.

The sacraments are outward signs and symbols; through them, the gospel is preached through divinely-ordained "pictures" of redemption. "Though fewer in number, and administered with more simplicity, and less outward glory" than the old ordinances, the New Testament sacraments hold forth Christ "in more fulness, evidence, and spiritual efficacy, to all nations, both Jews and Gentiles."[8] The Old Testament ordinances prefigured (in a typical manner) the Messiah who was yet to come; whereas the New Testament ordinances declare the work of Christ who has already come and conquered sin and death.

Since these signs are ordained by God, it should be clear that it is a monstrous presumption for anyone to add new sacraments, or to supplement the two sacraments of Christ with other "images" of human devising.[9] Yet, throughout history, men have often corrupted the church with liturgical "aids to worship" and

---

8. Westminster Confession of Faith, 7:6.

9. Among evangelicals, we have often heard it argued that we need "pictures of Jesus" to instruct children and other unlearned people. If individuals sense the need for visible representations of divine truth, we suggest they study the lawful administration of the sacraments. In baptism and the Lord's Supper (rightly observed) they will find divinely-ordained, outward representations of the essential truths of redemption.

new ecclesiastical ordinances. Others have embellished the sacraments by imposing a superstitious manner of observing them – such as Romish baptismal rites or Anglican liturgical forms. These deviations are an insult to Christ, because they imply a deficiency in the scriptures, as though the sacraments of Christ are insufficient as signs and seals, and therefore require humanly-devised supplements to increase their effectiveness.

Prayer

Prayer is a basic element of worship, whether public or private. Throughout the Old Testament, prayer was freely offered in a variety of settings beyond the boundaries of the temple. Therefore, we should not be surprised to see Christians constantly resorting to prayer within congregational meetings. There are numerous examples of congregational prayer in the book of Acts (Acts 4:24-31; 6:6-7; 12:5; 13:3; 14:23; 16:13; 16:25; 20:36; 21:5). Apostolic injunctions repeatedly enjoin prayer (Phil. 4:6; Col. 4:2; 1 Thess. 5:17; 5:25; 2 Thess. 3:1; 1 Tim. 2:1-2, 8).

Other Practices of Worship

Based upon Acts 2:42, we have briefly noted several basic elements of public worship found in the New Testament: the reading and preaching of the word of God, the sacraments, and prayer. Readers may wonder – beyond the subjects mentioned in Acts 2 – are there additional elements of worship which continue from the Old Testament, or which have been instituted by Christ or the apostles?

From other passages of scripture, we learn that psalm-singing was a regular practice within the Christian church (1 Cor. 14:26; Matt. 26:30; Mark 14:26; Eph. 5:19; Col. 3:16). The Bible additionally provides a warrant for fasting, as well as special times of thanksgiving.[10]

---

10. In the New Testament narratives, there are several examples of temporary aspects of worship – practices which were suited to the transitional era of the apostles. Elsewhere, I have noted reasons why such apostolic "signs

Apostolic Warning

We cannot conclude our discussion of the New Testament without looking at Paul's warning to the Colossians. The apostle warns them not to be beguiled by religious ordinances which are merely "the commandments and doctrines of men" (Col. 2:18-22). He cautions that such ordinances "have indeed a shew of wisdom in will worship, and humility, and neglecting of the body, not in any honour to the satisfying of the flesh."

The religious ordinances in question impose a burden upon those who practice them, requiring a degree of "humility, and neglecting of the body." This kind of religious discipline might seem commendable, but it is only a show.

A key to understanding the root problem with these ordinances is in the expression "will worship," which is somewhat cryptic to modern readers. The Greek term here might be rendered "voluntary worship" or "arbitrary worship."[11] The gist is that these ordinances are forms of worship or religious service chosen by man (according to the will of man), not means chosen by God.

This is the essence of corrupt worship, when men seek to establish their own forms of religious service. We might call it *free-will worship*, since the advocates of man-made worship are claiming that men possess the right (or freedom) to institute acceptable means to worship God.

This passage was cited frequently by the Reformers in their struggles against the corrupt worship and burdensome ordinances of Roman Catholicism. The passage was again employed by Scottish Protestants and English Puritans to repel the impositions of the Anglican liturgy. Indeed, Paul's warning furnishes a sweeping indictment against all humanly-imposed forms of worship and religious ordinances.

---

and wonders" were never expected to be permanent elements of worship. See Kevin Reed, *Biblical Worship* (Dallas: Presbyterian Heritage, 1995), pp. 75-80.

11. ἐθελοθρησκεία – The Geneva Bible translates the term as "voluntary religion," with a note explaining it as "such as men have chosen according to their own fantasy." Tyndale renders it "chosen holiness."

In the twentieth century, many people act as though idolatry is a remote possibility. Yet, when we understand that the biblical condemnation of corrupt worship extends to all man-made forms or worship, we see the need of the apostolic admonition, "Little children, keep yourselves from idols (1 John 5:21)."

Summary

Based upon the teaching of scripture, we derive the following truths respecting worship:

1. God is the only proper recipient of worship.
2. Mankind must worship the LORD only according to the means prescribed by God.
3. It is sinful to amend or alter the worship prescribed by God in his word.
4. There is no longer a central place for worship. The temple ordinances have reached fulfillment.
5. The sacrificial ordinances have reached their conclusion; the finished work of Christ means that sacrificial ordinances are no longer to be conducted as part of stated public worship.
6. There is therefore no need for a new sacrificial priesthood.
7. The ordinary elements of worship now include: prayer, the reading, preaching, and hearing of God's word; singing of psalms; and the right administration of the sacraments – as well as occasional appointments of fasting and thanksgiving.

The Worship of Rome

The centerpiece of Romish worship, the Mass, is blatant idolatry. Rome holds to the doctrine of transubstantiation, contending that the bread and wine are transformed into the actual body and blood of Christ. The Mass is believed to be an actual sacrifice, possessing propitiatory merits. The elements of bread and wine are uplifted, where they may be adored (worshipped) by the assembled congregation. The people share only in the wafer, for the cup is withheld from the laity. This "sacrifice" of the Mass, with its ceremonial priesthood, is utter blasphemy against the finished priestly work of Christ. The Mass is a gross corruption of the Lord's Supper.

Romish edifices for worship are filled with graven images: pictures and statues made to depict the Lord, Mary, the apostles and the saints. Rome claims that these images serve a didactic purpose, and that the images may properly be venerated. Moreover, popish religious orders and merchants peddle a multitude of religious artifacts which promote superstition among the people.

Rome has expanded from two to seven the number of sacraments, and added a multitude of ecclesiastical rites, including clerical attire, the ecclesiastical year, and symbolic rituals for hosts of religious observations. The word of God is crowded out by liturgy, images, and ritual. Additionally, like the Pharisees, Rome has a multitude of religious ordinances which stand as a symbol of her false piety. Imposed clerical celibacy is a prime example of an ecclesiastical ordinance which contravenes biblical doctrine.

Repeated and regular attendance at the Mass and other Romish rituals is patent disobedience to the scriptural commands for Christians to avoid idolatry. Anyone who knowingly retains a connection with this Romish worship cannot maintain a credible profession of faith, for the Bible says: "What agreement hath the temple of God with idols? ... Wherefore come out from among them, and be ye separate, saith the Lord, and touch not the unclean thing; and I will receive you...." (2 Cor. 6:16-17).

The issue of Rome's idolatry was at the heart of the Reformation. "For [John] Calvin the worship of the medieval church had become 'gross idolatry.' The issue of idolatry was for him as serious as the issue of works-righteousness in justification. Both represented a pandering to human proclivities, rather than desiring to please and obey God. Calvin insists that no unity can exist in worship with idolaters."[12]

---

12. W. Robert Godfrey"What Really Caused the Great Divide?" in John Armstrong, ed., *Roman Catholicism: Evangelicals Analyze What Divides and Unites Us* (Chicago: Moody Press, 1994), p. 72. Godfrey makes several references to Calvin's tract on *The Necessity of Reforming the Church* (1544); a

The Worship of Evangelicalism

While evangelicals do not celebrate the Mass (not yet, at least), many take comfort in a relative comparison with Rome, noting that their worship is not as degenerate as the idolatry of the Mass. But relative comparisons are not to be the measure of true religion. The Bible condemns any form of man-made worship as a species of idolatry; and evangelical churches are full of synthetic worship. The latest fads include lavish musical performances, drama, puppet shows, films, sacred dance, and heretical hymns – to name but a few infractions. Much as with Rome, the word of God is crowded out, in this case by entertainment, multi-media presentations, and false teaching.

Evangelical edifices and instructional materials are filled with graven images of the Lord. In recent years, many evangelicals have promoted "missionary" activities through the use of the *Jesus* film, which is available in multiple languages. Evangelicals claim that these images serve a didactic purpose, especially for teaching children and evangelizing the unlearned. Their argument is merely a modern paraphrase of the old popish claim that images serve well as "books for the laity."[13] On the contrary, "faith cometh by hearing, and hearing by *the word* of God" (Rom. 10:17).

Readers are invited to take a stroll through a typical evangelical bookstore. The shelves are filled with religious trinkets and paraphernalia which rival popish merchants, and may even exceed them for sheer tackiness.

---

new edition of this important work by Calvin has been reprinted recently by Protestant Heritage Press, P. O. Box 180922, Dallas, Texas 75218. For an important study respecting the reformers' views on worship, see: Carlos M. N. Eire, *War Against the Idols: The Reformation of Worship from Erasmus to Calvin* (Cambridge: Cambridge University Press, 1986). Eire demonstrates that the reformers' struggle against idolatry was a central facet of the Protestant Reformation.

13. "*But may not images be tolerated in the churches, as books to the laity?* No: for we must not pretend to be wiser than God, who will have his people taught, not by dumb images, but by the lively preaching of his word" (2 Tim. 3:16; 2 Pet. 1:19; Jer. 10:1. etc.; Hab. 2:19-19). Heidelberg Catechism #98.

There is also a disturbing trend among evangelicals to be fascinated with Romish ritual and liturgy. This trend is not isolated to "high-church" communions, such as the Anglican and "orthodox" churches which were never thoroughly reformed. Rather, some "Protestant" churches have begun adopting the trappings of Romish rites and liturgy: ministers don priestly gowns and begin introducing elements of liturgical worship. Churches post crosses in prominent places within their buildings, and begin following the ecclesiastical year of Rome.

Biblical psalm-singing is noticeably absent throughout evangelicalism. Instead, contemporary evangelicals seem to relish sentimental ditties and heretical hymns. Many who never sing the psalms will unite in singing "Faith of Our Fathers," oblivious to the fact that the hymn's author composed it as a testimony of his own conversion to Rome![14] Perhaps it is fitting, since these modern evangelical choristers are on a parallel pilgrimage.

Evangelicals have also mutilated the sacraments. Whereas Rome corrupts the Lord's Supper and withholds the cup from the laity, many evangelical congregations dispense neither element to the people. In some cases, the biblical elements of the Lord's supper have been replaced by grape juice and crackers (or coffee cake). The idea that a local congregation has the right to change the elements given by the Lord is every bit as pernicious

---

14. Frederick W. Faber was ordained in the Church of England in 1842. Under the influence of John Henry Newman, he entered the Roman Catholic church in 1846. Three years later, Faber published a book, *Jesus and Mary; or Catholic Hymns for Singing and Reading.* The third stanza of this hymn is often altered in evangelical hymnals; the original text reads:

> Faith of our fathers! Mary's prayers
> Shall win our country back to thee;
> And through the truth that comes from God,
> England shall then indeed be free.
> Faith of our fathers, holy faith!
> We would be true to thee till death.

Cited from: William Jensen Reynolds, *Hymns of Our Faith* (Nashville: Broadman, 1964), pp. 43, 289.

as Rome's doctrine of church power. It makes little difference whether divine authority is usurped by a priestly hierarchy (Rome) or a localized democracy (evangelicalism); in either case it is an arrogant presumption against the *sola scriptura* rule of biblical religion.

In the previous chapter we mentioned the altar call in connection with spurious evangelism. The altar call also impacts the doctrine of worship because it functions as a sacrament – as a public "sign and seal" of grace. Like Rome, evangelicals have man-made religious ordinances which stand as symbols of false piety and worship.[15]

Conclusion

Both Rome and modern evangelicalism share an underlying assumption that the church has power to innovate in worship. A contrast exists in outward practices because Rome's innovations flow from centuries of accumulated traditions; whereas evangelicals often discard tradition in favour of "contemporary" practices in worship. At root, however, both groups share the assumption that men have the right to supplement the biblical means of worship.

As we have examined the subject of worship, we have noted many similarities between Rome and evangelicals. It is a startling to realize how the worship of God has been corrupted by both evangelicals and Roman Catholics together.

---

15. Another example, which has waned in popularity in the broader evangelical community, is the way some fundamentalists measure a man's piety by whether he totally abstains from all alcoholic beverages.

Chapter 4

The Marks of the Church

THE PROTESTANT Reformation presented people with many serious issues. We have looked at the chief questions: (1.) What is the right way of salvation, and (2.) What is the right way to worship God? There was yet another query which follows upon the heels of these questions: Which is the true church?[1]

Both Rome and Protestants claimed to be the true church, each denouncing the other as a false church. Additionally, there were Anabaptists and other sects which condemned both Rome and Protestant congregations as false churches. Today, the problem is exacerbated by a myriad of religious assemblies, all claiming the title of Christ's church. How should a man sift through these conflicting claims? How can he know which church he should join?

The reformers were sensitive to this dilemma, and the creedal formulations of Protestants addressed the issue in a strongly pastoral manner. The creeds hearken back to those basic issues we have already examined: the way of worship, and the way of salvation. From scripture, the reformers concluded that we should look for three basic marks to identify the true church: (1.) the preaching of the gospel, (2.) the proper administration of the sacraments,

---

1. In the following discussion, our comments are narrowly focused upon the identity of the true church in an institutional sense. Because the believer's connection to the institutional church comes within the context of the local congregation, that is the focal point of our inquiry.

In an enlarged discussion of related themes, we could explore the differences between the visible church and the invisible church. The scriptures clearly make a distinction between the *universal* church of all ages, the elect, – "the heavenly Jerusalem … the general assembly and church of the firstborn, which are written in heaven" (Heb. 12:22-23) – and the local congregations which are composed of those in outward communion with the assemblies of

(3.) the right exercise of church discipline.[2] Where these three marks are clearly present, we may rest assured we have found the church of the Lord Jesus Christ.[3]

In a most practical manner, these marks provide the believer with a measure by which to evaluate a local congregation before joining it. If the marks are conspicuous, we may join with a clear conscience, knowing it to be a genuine Christian congregation. If these three marks are not plainly manifest, we should look elsewhere; we are not obligated to join an assembly which does not exhibit the marks of a true church.

Further, if it is obvious that the opposite marks are present – such as a false gospel, corruption of the sacraments and worship, and gross abuse or neglect of church discipline – then it is our duty to avoid such an assembly and admonish others to do likewise. Such openly corrupt assemblies are synagogues of Satan.

It is not our purpose to enter into a detailed discussion of each of the individual marks. As a summary, we note the following facts.

"Faith cometh by hearing, and hearing by the word of God" (Rom. 10:17). If a religious assembly has not the gospel of Christ,

---

Christ. Thus, the historic Protestant creeds distinguish between the *visible* church and the *invisible* church (cf. Westminster Confession (1646), chapter 25; the Scottish Confession of Faith (1560), chapters 16 and 18). Obviously our discussion pertains mainly to the visible church, regarding its proper identification: that is, how it may be discerned among local congregations.

2. The marks of the church are treated in The Confession of the English Congregation at Geneva (1556), the French Confession of Faith (1559), articles 26-28; the Scottish Confession of Faith (1560), chapters 16 and 18, and the Belgic Confession of Faith (1561), articles 27-29; Second Helvetic Confession (1566), chapter 17.

3. The Westminster Confession elaborates on the doctrine of the church when it says, "The purest churches under heaven are subject both to mixture and error; and some have so degenerated as to become no churches of Christ, but synagogues of Satan" (25:5).This statement does not purport to tell us how we may "rate" churches in a dubious condition, nor does the Confession commend believers to "less pure" churches which have not yet fully degenerated into synagogues of Satan. Rather, the Westminster Confession lets

it is not worthy to be called a church. Without the gospel, there can be no true Christians; without true Christians, there can be no real church.

The administration of the sacraments is an indicator of a congregation's practices in worship. If an assembly substitutes man-made forms of worship in place of the sacraments, it is not worthy to be regarded as a true church. And when a congregation adopts a multitude of humanly-devised "aids to worship," as supplements to the biblical ordinances, the leaven of idolatry is already present. Christians must avoid corrupt worship, "for what agreement hath the temple of God with idols?" (2 Cor. 6:16).

Church discipline is designed to maintain the glory of God and preserve the health of the church. If a person makes a profession of faith, but exhibits a life of moral corruption, men regard his profession as hypocrisy. Similarly, if an assembly claims the title of a church, while tolerating notorious heresies and scandals in its midst, it has degenerated so as to become no church of Christ, but a "synagogue of Satan" (Rev. 2:9; 3:9).

We stress that the marks of the church are used to answer a question about the legitimacy of religious assemblies in their *collective* capacity. Does the congregation corporately bear the character of a genuine church of Christ? The failure of a congregation jointly to measure up to these standards does not, in itself, consign every individual there to flames of perdition.

---

stand the previous creedal doctrine that calls upon men to seek out a true church – one clearly discerned by the right marks.

These comments would seem to be unnecessary, were it not for modern Presbyterians who have sought to pit the Westminster Confession against the previous Protestant creeds, in order to lessen the role of the marks of the church. It should be noted that it was the Church of Scotland which ratified the Westminster Standards, giving the standards their ecclesiastical approval. Yet nowhere in the acts of ratification did the Scottish church repudiate its former creedal testimony. It is worth noting that the Scottish General Assembly had previously ratified (among others) all each of the following creeds: The Confession of the English Congregation at Geneva, the French Confession, and the Scottish Confession of 1560; and all of these creeds affirm the marks of the true church.

Having said that, we must assert the obligation of every Christian to seek out a true congregation. Believers are admonished not to forsake "the assembling of ourselves together, as the manner of some is" (Heb. 10:25). The Reformers took this duty seriously, noting "that it is important to discern with care and prudence which is the true church, for this title has been much abused."[4] "It is the duty of all believers, according to the word of God, to separate themselves from all those who do not belong to the church, and to join themselves to this congregation [the true church], wheresoever God hath established it.... Therefore all those, who separate themselves from the same, or do not join themselves to it, act contrary to the ordinance of God."[5]

It is the office of every believer to discern between true and false shepherds. Christ "putteth forth his own sheep, he goeth before them, and the sheep follow him: for they know his voice. *And a stranger they will not follow,* but will flee from him: for they know not the voice of strangers" (John 10:4-5). Since the preaching of an assembly reveals its doctrine of the gospel, the believer must evaluate the teaching ministry of the congregation. Is this *church* faithfully proclaiming the word of Christ? The discernment of the believer is tested in this regard, and by his decision respecting church membership. Will *he* follow the voice of Christ,

---

4. French Confession of Faith (1559), article 27. The Belgic Confession (1561) says, "We believe that we ought diligently and circumspectly to discern from the Word of God which is the true Church, since all the sects which are in the world assume to themselves the name of the Church" (article 29). The Scottish Confession says, "Because that Satan from the beginning has laboured to deck his pestilent synagogue with the title of the kirk of God, and has inflamed the hearts of cruel murderers to persecute, trouble, and molest the true kirk and members thereof ... it is a thing most requisite that the true kirk be discerned from the filthy synagogue, by clear and perfect notes, lest we, being deceived, receive and embrace to our own condemnation the one for the other" (chapter 18).

5. Belgic Confession, article 28. In some cases, there may not be a preexisting true congregation near a believer's home. Still, the imperative to separate from false churches remains. In such irregular circumstances, where there is not an acceptable preexisting church, the believer would be encour-

or will he entertain the voice of a stranger by joining a corrupt church?

These principles have great relevance to the present interaction between Protestants, evangelicals, and Roman Catholics. Yet the imperative nature of proper church membership is studiously avoided in contemporary literature on inter-denominational relations. We contend that a proper approach to church membership is mandatory for those who are faithful to the Lord and his word. The marks of a true church will dictate two crucial matters: (1.) what church we will join; (2) and whether we should recognize a particular communion as a legitimate church and account its membership outwardly as brethren in the Lord.

Roman Catholicism and the Marks of the Church

Having considered the marks of a true church, in light of our earlier examination of the gospel and true worship, we must conclude that Roman Catholicism is a false church. At the Council of Trent, Rome officially repudiated the biblical doctrine of justification, institutionally cutting itself off from the true gospel. The popish corruption of the gospel and the sacraments, and Rome's blatant practices of idolatry, openly display its character as a synagogue of Satan.[6] There obviously is no biblical discipline, because

---

aged to help form one or, perhaps, move to a location near a true congregation. During the Reformation, Protestants formed numerous "house churches" sometimes called *privy congregations,* and often held "underground" meetings. (See Second Helvetic Confession, chapter 17.)

The present author has discussed ecclesiastical polity in more detail elsewhere. See: Kevin Reed, *Biblical Church Government* (Dallas: Presbyterian Heritage, 1983, 1994 expanded edition); also, *Presbyterian Government in Extraordinary Times* (Dallas: privately published [loose-leaf], 1993).

6. "Therefore we condemn the papal assemblies, as the pure word of God is banished from them, their sacraments are corrupted, or falsified, or destroyed, and all superstitions and idolatries are in them. We hold, then that all who take part in these acts, and commune in that church, separate and cut themselves off from the body of Christ...." (French Confession, article 28) "As for the false church, she ascribes more power and authority to herself and her ordinances than to the word of God, and will not submit herself to the

the heresies and corruptions of Rome go unchecked, while anathemas are hurled against those who profess the scriptural gospel.

One recent writer, William Webster, makes an appeal to Roman Catholics to "come out from among them and be separate" (2 Cor. 6:17). "Why do I say that?" he asks. "Am I being impolitic in this counsel, especially when many evangelicals are saying we should *not* call upon Catholics to leave their communion?" He goes on to say, "The issues that separate Protestants and Roman Catholics are not minor. They are major. They have to do with the eternal destinies of men and women."[7] These comments speak volumes at a time when many evangelical churchmen have lost sight of the pastoral urgency of calling men to repentance.

Evangelicalism and the Marks of the Church

But again, we must not stop with Rome. As we have seen, many modern evangelical churches have embraced the false gospel of decisionalism and adopted man-made worship. Moreover, great heresies and scandals remain unremedied within evangelical congregations; because church discipline is so unpopular among the people, it is generally avoided. In short, if the marks of the church are telling against Rome, they are equally telling against evangelicalism.

---

yoke of Christ. Neither does she administer the sacraments as appointed by Christ in his word, but adds to and takes from them, as she thinks proper; she relieth more upon men than upon Christ; and persecutes those, who live holily according to the word of God, and rebuke her for her errors, covetousness, and idolatry" (Belgic Confession, article 29). The Confession of the English Congregation speaks of "idolaters and heretics, as Papists, Anabaptists, with suchlike limbs of Antichrist."

7. William Webster, "Did I Really Leave the Holy Catholic Church?" in *Roman Catholicism: Evangelical Protestants Analyze What Divides and Unites Us* (edited by John Armstrong; Chicago: Moody Press 1994), p. 286, 288. Webster adds: "I believe that a Roman Catholic who is sincerely committed to following truth will eventually leave the Roman Catholic Church, realizing as the Reformers taught that it is not *the* historic, biblical, holy, catholic church" (p. 286).

In a recent evangelical book on Roman Catholicism, Donald Bloesch flatly denies the historic distinction between true and false churches.[8] Another author in the same book, Michael Horton, makes a passing reference to the marks of the church (leaving out the third mark on discipline), stating that Rome is "not a true visible church."[9] Later in the same essay, Horton criticizes evangelicals for Pelagian evangelism: "Entire denominations that were committed confessionally to the doctrine of justification [by grace alone through faith alone] have ended up adopting, in actual practice, a Pelagian message. When evangelicals deny human depravity and inability, affirm that human beings cooperate in their own conversion by the use of their free will, and view salvation as a project of moral improvement (especially when that affirms a notion of entire sanctification), they are further afield from the gospel than Rome has ever been."[10] One might expect the author to state the implications of his observations, and discuss the marks of the church as they relate to evangelicals. But the essay comes to an abrupt halt, without following through on such important ramifications.

Earlier in the same book, Robert Godfrey correctly summarizes John Calvin's analysis of the chief disputes between Rome and the Protestants: namely the conflicts respecting the gospel and true worship. After his historical overview, Godfrey asks, "Were Calvin to evaluate Rome today … what would he conclude?" He rightly answers that Calvin "would surely conclude that Rome is

8. "It has been fashionable in evangelical Protestantism to regard the Reformation church as the true church of Christ and the Roman Catholic church as a false church. A more biblical stance is to see one holy and apostolic church irremediably fractured by the Reformation." Donald Bloesch, "Is Spirituality Enough?" in *Roman Catholicism: Evangelical Protestants Analyze What Divides and Unites Us* (edited by John Armstrong; Chicago: Moody Press 1994), p. 152.

9. Michael Horton, "What Still Keeps Us Apart?" in *Roman Catholicism: Evangelical Protestants Analyze What Divides and Unites Us* (edited by John Armstrong; Chicago: Moody Press 1994), p. 247; 258.

10. Michael Horton, "What Still Keeps Us Apart?" p. 263.

worse off today than it was in the sixteenth century." Godfrey then reminds us of Rome's "syncretistic" worship, doctrine of justification that "still rests on human cooperation," and administration of the sacraments "in an idolatrous and magical manner."

Curiously, Godfrey adds, "Calvin would no doubt equally lament the sad state of much of Protestantism today." Considering that Godfrey's essay is included in a book styling its authors as "evangelical Protestants," his definition of Protestantism must include the evangelicals of our time. So why does Godfrey let evangelicals off with only a mild critique, in comparison to his pointed criticisms of Rome? Surely what is good for the Popish goose should be good for the evangelical gander. Why not apply the same historic measures to both Rome and evangelicalism?[11]

One suspects that contemporary evangelical writers are reticent to press the issue more forcefully because of the embarrassing implications. A due regard for the marks of the church would not only unchurch Rome, but a major part of modern evangelicalism. That prospect is so startling, that even the most conservative and "reformed" theologians in our day cannot bring themselves to consider the idea.

Horton speaks with hope of a new reformation within Protestantism.[12] But if there is to be a new reformation, we need to come clean on the depth of the problem among evangelicals, and summon them to repent, believe the true gospel, and depart from their idols in worship. (Anything less is simply beating around the bush.) And until evangelicals bring forth such fruits meet for repentance, historic Protestants will have no choice but to regard the bulk of evangelical churches as no more legitimate than Rome. Once again, we see that evangelicals and Roman Catholics together are making shipwreck of the faith.

---

11. W. Robert Godfrey, "What Really Caused the Great Divide?" in *Roman Catholicism: Evangelical Protestants Analyze What Divides and Unites Us* (edited by John Armstrong; Chicago: Moody Press 1994), p. 79.

12. Michael Horton, "What Still Keeps Us Apart?" p. 264.

Chapter 5

What is an Evangelical?

BEFORE going any further, we need to address a problem of nomenclature: What is an evangelical? After all, when people call themselves Catholics, they generally mean that they are members of the Romish communion joined to the papacy. But when people call themselves evangelicals, the designation does not denote affiliation with any particular denomination or creedal formula. So what is an evangelical? How should we define the word?

"The word evangelicalism derives from the Greek *euangellismos*. The evangel is the good news or gospel, and throughout the New Testament it designates the message of salvation. Paul was not ashamed of this gospel, and throughout the New Testament it designates the message of salvation. Paul was not ashamed of this gospel, for 'it is the power of God for salvation to everyone who has faith, to the Jew first and also to the Greek' (Rom. 1:16). Because it was the message, the indispensable message of salvation, the Apostle pronounced the curse of God upon those who preached any other evangel whether himself or an angel from heaven (Gal. 1:8)."[1]

Historically, the term *evangelical* was used to designate a person's association with specific views about the *evangel*, the gospel. During the reformation, the term identified those who held to the evangelical proclamation of the reformers: that is, the

1. John H. Gerstner, "The Theological Boundaries of Evangelical Faith," in *The Evangelicals: What They Believe, Who They Are, Where They Are Changing* (Abingdon: Nashville, 1975), p. 22. The A.V. renders Rom. 1:16, "it is the power of God unto salvation to every one that believeth; to the Jew first, and also to the Greek."

term referred to Protestants.[2] The popish detractors of Protestants sometimes called them "gospellers" – another term which points to the *content* of the Protestant faith.[3]

Now, as we have already shown, the theology of the reformation was based upon the gospel of God's sovereign grace in saving sinners. Mankind is dead in trespasses: men bear the guilt of sin and are dominated by the power of sin; they are totally incapable of contributing to their own deliverance from either the guilt or power of sin. Justification comes by grace, based upon Christ's merit alone, received by faith alone. Sanctification follows as a separate but related process, whereby the redeemed sinner progressively grows in practical godliness.

Since reformation doctrine is simply a statement of the biblical evangel; and since contemporary evangelicalism generally rejects this doctrine of sovereign grace; then it follows that modern evangelicalism isn't really *evangelical* at all, according to this historic usage of the term.

John Gerstner summarizes the historical progression of the term: "As used in the Bible then, the term *euangellismos* refers to the way of salvation and was so understood subsequently. At the Reformation it came into prominent usage precisely because the

2. 'Despite the dominant usage of *euangellismos* in the New Testament, its derivative, evangelical, was not widely or controversially employed until the Reformation period. Then it came into prominence with Martin Luther precisely because he reasserted Paul's teaching on the *euangellismos* as the indispensable message of salvation. Its light, he argued, was hidden under a bushel of ecclesiastical authority, tradition, and liturgy. The essence of the saving message for Luther was justification by faith alone, the article by which not only the church stands or falls but each individual as well. Erasmus, Thomas More, and Johannes Eck denigrated those who accepted this view and referred to them as "evangelicals." ' John H. Gerstner, "The Theological Boundaries of Evangelical Faith," p. 23.

3. The term *Protestant* itself is derived from the Latin word *protestari,* which means to *witness, confess* or *testify.* The idea is one of giving a public testimony to the truths of the Christian faith. Once again, we see the Protestant reformers were described by a term which points to their *content* of their faith.

Roman Church seemed to Protestants to have lost the gospel way of salvation. In the reformers' formulation and well into the nineteenth century, evangelism was God's way of salvation, not only in the offering of it to men but in the applying of it to their hearts as well. Last century, however, the evangel began to be seen more as the divine offer of grace and not so much as the divine application of grace."[4]

The term *evangelical* has undergone a further shift in usage, in that it is now commonly used to describe a *shared experience*, instead of a common commitment to a body of doctrine. In previous centuries, the term pointed objectively to a set of beliefs, a body of truth concerning redemption, held by Protestants. Most "conservative" Protestants no longer hold these doctrines; but large numbers of these "conservative" non-Catholics have had an emotional religious experience; further, they possess a zeal for sharing their experience with others.[5] The common denominator of experience becomes the bond of unity, and it cuts across denominational boundaries, making creedal differences largely

---

4. John H. Gerstner, "The Theological Boundaries of Evangelical Faith," p. 35. See chapter 1 above. Also note Gerstner's statement regarding 20th-century evangelicalism. It has "lost some important aspects of its Reformation heritage, especially as these relate to the doctrines of grace, the depth of human depravity, and the indispensable need of God's saving initiative not only in sending his Son, Jesus Christ, to accomplish salvation but also in inclining sinners to accept it" (p. 31).

5. The experience is often said to be that of the new birth, or conversion. The "testimonies" of these evangelicals usually revolve around the pivotal moment of their "decision," regardless of whether the decision was made at a mass rally, in a one-on-one conversation, or as a result of some other provocative event (or events).

As we have noted earlier, the modern conception of conversion is radically different from the biblical position of the Protestant reformers. We firmly hold to the necessity of the new birth, and rejoice in the news of a sinner's true conversion to God. But the momentous conversion of a sinner genuinely occurs only by the sovereign operations of God's Spirit, in connection with the true gospel.

irrelevant to those who share a similar religious experience.[6] Thus the term *evangelical* has shifted from an *objective* focus to a purely *subjective* one.

The problem of definition is clouded by modern writers, like Keith Fournier, who wish to extend the term *evangelical* even further, to include Roman Catholics. Fournier writes in a congenial manner. He uses lingo popular among evangelicals.[7] Nevertheless, he candidly states, "I am a Roman Catholic, not by accident or mistake but by heartfelt conviction."[8]

Fournier's theological convictions become apparent as he takes the reader through a meandering description of his personal experiences. During his narrative, he endorses many of Roman Catholicism's distinctive doctrines and practices: justification as a process, transubstantiation and the sacrifice of the Mass, baptismal regeneration, praying before images, free will and denial of human inability, charismatic experiences, the rosary and devotion to Mary.

---

6. Gerstner says, "Others may imagine that anyone who shows religious earnestness, regardless of his views, or who engages in evangelism, regardless of the evangel which he preaches, can be called an evangelical. Those who have self-consciously assumed this title, however, insist that they have done so on account of their theology." John H. Gerstner, "The Theological Boundaries of Evangelical Faith," p. 33

The present writer is not convinced of Gerstner's last assertion. As we contend in portions of this chapter, evangelicals often see themselves more in the *subjective* terms of their religious experience, than in the *objective* terms of their theology. The attitude Gerstner rebuts has become all too much the norm. Anyone with religious zeal, even if he preaches an heretical evangel, is warmly accepted *as* an evangelical *by* other evangelicals.

7. Fournier speaks of conversion, using the expression, 'inviting "Yeshua," Jesus, God's Son into my heart to be my Savior.' *Evangelical Catholics* (Nashville: Thomas Nelson, 1990), pp. 33-34; cf. p. 41. Even here, he doesn't mean exactly the same thing as most evangelicals, since Fournier views conversion as an ongoing process (see p. 15), whereas evangelicals employ the term to describe a one-time event.

8. *Evangelical Catholics*, p. 59.

When Fournier recounts preachers and scholars of the past, he jumps from medieval figures to later figures such as Wesley, Finney, Loyola, C.S. Lewis, and Billy Graham. Fournier's omission of the Protestant reformers from his list of great men of the faith is quite telling. Early in his book, Fournier mentions *reading* some of the writings of the reformers. But he reserves his *praise* for others, especially papal mystics and heretical "Protestants" (such as Finney, Wesley, Graham, Lewis).

Fournier's agenda is clearly popish. His ecumenism does not extend to participation in non-Romish administration of the sacraments. At one point he states: "As a Catholic Christian, I believe the Eucharist is the sacrament of unity. And because the church is divided, I embrace my church's position that I cannot participate in the Eucharist with Christians of other traditions. We are not one. We must long to be one, and it should grieve our hearts that we cannot go to a common table.... We cannot pretend there aren't differences in our understandings of the Eucharist, or the Lord's Supper. There are differences, and they are real and important." Earlier in the book, he says, "I believe it would be ingenuine for believers who do not agree on the real presence of Christ in the Eucharist to join this sacrament of unity. I long for the day when it will be possible for all Christians to share this sacred meal either here or in the wedding feast of heaven, which it symbolizes."[9] Thus, the eventual unity envisioned by Fournier will only be achieved if evangelicals accept Rome's terms of surrender, and join in the corrupt worship of popery.

Throughout his writings, Fournier uses a tactic that most evangelicals will find disarming. He employs the lingo of evangelicals and uses language calculated to soften the contrast between Protestants and Romanists. As we shall see in the next chapter, this tactic is also exhibited in the document, "Evangelicals and Catholics Together."

Readers should not be fooled by such an approach. William Cunningham, the eminent 19th-century Scottish theologian, has

9. *Evangelical Catholics*, pp. 161, 17.

remarked: "There are two different and opposite lines of policy which Romish controversialists have pursued upon this subject [justification], according as seemed to be most expedient for their interests at the time. Sometimes they have represented the doctrine of the Reformers upon the subject of justification as something hideous and monstrous – as overturning the foundations of all morality, and fitted only to produce universal wickedness and profligacy; and at other times they have affected a willingness to listen to the grounds on which Protestants defend themselves from this charge, to admit that these grounds are not altogether destitute of weight, and that, consequently, there is not so great a difference between their doctrine in substance and that of the Church of Rome. They then enlarge upon the important influence which the alleged errors of the Church of Rome on the subject of justification had in producing the Reformation – quote some of the passages which show the paramount importance which the first Reformers attached to this subject – and proceed to draw the inference that the Reformation was founded upon misrepresentation and calumny, since it appears, and has been admitted even by learned Protestants, that the errors of the Church of Rome, even if they were to admit for the sake of argument that she had erred, are not nearly so important as the Reformers had represented them to be."[10]

The appropriation of the term evangelical by religious special-interest groups has further exacerbated the problem of definition.[11] Has the term lost all connection to its historical usage? So

10. William Cunningham, *Historical Theology,* (1862; rpt. Edinburgh: Banner of Truth, 1979), vol. 2, pp. 4-5.

11. "As evangelicalism has continued to grow numerically, it has seeped through its older structures and now spills out in all directions, producing a family of hybrids whose theological connections are quite baffling: evangelical Catholics, evangelicals who are Catholic, evangelical liberationists, evangelical feminists, evangelical ecumenists, ecumenists who are evangelical, young evangelicals, orthodox evangelicals, radical evangelicals, liberal evangelicals, Liberals who are evangelical, and charismatic evangelicals. The word *evangelical,* precisely because it has lost its confessional dimension, has

it seems. The result is that the term *evangelical* is utterly meaningless, unless an author clearly indicates how he is using the word.[12]

The present author has wrestled with the problem of definition while preparing this essay, and I have generally restricted my criticisms to self-styled evangelicals. While some criticisms will not apply to all individuals who regard themselves as evangelicals, there is abundant evidence to illustrate the sad factors which are sinking the ship of contemporary evangelicalism.

---

become descriptively anemic. To say that someone is an evangelical says little about what they are likely to believe (although it says more if they are older and less if they are younger). And so the term is forced to compensate for its theological weakness by borrowing meaning from adjectives the very presence of which signals the fragmentation and disintegration of the movement. What is now primary is not what is evangelical but what is adjectivally distinctive, whether Catholic, liberationist, feminist, ecumenist, young, orthodox, radical, liberal, or charismatic. It is, I believe, the dark prelude to death, when parasites have finally succeeded in bringing down their host. Amid the clamor of all these new models of evangelical faith there is the sound of a death rattle." David F. Wells, *No Place for Truth, or, Whatever Happened to Evangelical Theology* (Grand Rapids: Eerdmans, 1993), p. 134.

12. Yale historian Sydney Ahlstrom has noted there is no "uniformity of usage for this sacred and solemn term...." He states that no single usage has been normative, so that "historians who sail these seas have been as helplessly caught in the currents of popular usage as the humblest fisherman." In a footnote, Ahlstrom illustrates the "difficulties of definition" with a brief summary of contemporary evangelical authors: '[Bernard] Ramm praises Scholastic Orthodoxy, tends to reject modern thought ... and yet speaks of 35 to 40 million evangelicals located almost everywhere. Bloesch calls evangelicalism a "mood," yet names nine hallmarks and then undoes that sign of precision by throwing out dozens of names from St. Theresa of Avila to Bonhoeffer. Shelley, as an historian of the National Association of Evangelicals, is more inclusive than Ramm, less eclectic than Bloesch, and more inclined to stress "a true decision for Christ." Bloesch somewhat confusingly speaks of a new evangelicalism replacing the old "Neo-Evangelicalism of the forties and fifties.... All three distance themselves to varying degrees from fundamentalism, but do not exclude it.' Sydney Ahlstrom, "From Puritanism to Evangelicalism: A Critical Perspective," in *The Evangelicals: What They Believe, Who They Are, Where They Are Changing* (Abingdon: Nashville, 1975), pp. 269-70, 288 (note 1).

"Evangelicals and Catholics Together"

WE COME NOW to a brief consideration of the document entitled, "Evangelicals and Catholics Together" (ECT).[1] The largest section of the document, under the heading of "We Contend Together," urges cooperation between Romanists and evangelicals on a wide range of social and political issues, dealing with religious freedom, abortion,[2] pornography, parental choice in education, a market economy, and appreciation of Western culture. Collaboration on these issues is obviously what has built support for the document among both Roman Catholics and evangelicals.

Interwoven with the social and political issues, however, the ECT document contains false theological presuppositions and blatant compromises with Romish doctrine. Protestants who sign this document for political purposes will find that they have given away the store.

Gospel Issues

The introduction of ECT enunciates a basic premise underlying the document: "As Christ is one, so the Christian mission is one. That one mission can be and should be advanced in diverse ways." Later, the authors assert, "We are called and we are therefore re-

1. This document has been reproduced in numerous places. In our quotations from ECT, references to the document include the section title, followed by sequential numbering of paragraphs within the section.

2. Evangelicals are right to denounce abortion as murder and to call abortionists to repentance. Since pro-life evangelicals oppose those who murder the body, why do they not equally abhor those who seek to murder the soul (such as the exponents of popish religion)?

solved to explore patterns of working and witnessing together in order to advance the mission of Christ."[3] Can Protestants have a common mission with Romanists, when they are still disagreed over the content of the gospel? The issue of justification by faith has not been resolved (something acknowledged within the ECT document itself). Moreover, there are a myriad of other issues related to the gospel, such as the nature of faith and divine sovereignty in the conversion of sinners. If these are not spelled out clearly, how can there be any talk of a common effort in fulfilling the great commission? In this case, the allusion to "diverse ways" seems to be a veiled reference to diverse gospels. The attitude is quite different from that of the apostle Paul in Galatians 1.[4]

The document affirms "that we are justified by grace through faith because of Christ."[5] The important term that is missing in that sentence is the word *alone*, as in the historic Protestant affirmation of justification by faith alone. In fact, when the document later provides a lists of unresolved issues between Romanists and evangelicals, the subject of justification is made conspicuous precisely because it is absent from that list.

Speaking of missionary zeal, the document makes one of its rare allusions to scripture, "How shall they hear without a

3. "Introduction," 3rd and 10th paragraphs.

4. In a schizophrenic moment, the authors say, "The achievement of good will and cooperation between Evangelicals and Catholics must not be at the price of the urgency and clarity of the Christian witness to the gospel" ("We Witness Together," paragraph 1). Keep in mind that the authors previously provided a list of unresolved differences between Romanists and Evangelicals, and the list touched some very significant issues: differences pertaining to *sola scriptura*, the nature of the church, worship, and baptismal regeneration. In spite of these unresolved differences, they press on with the assertion that their alliance to "witness together" must not come at the price of the "urgency and clarity of the Christian witness to the gospel." Such reckless statements are mind boggling (or mind numbing) when one begins to reflect on their ramifications. Apparently the authors do not believe that such issues as scriptural authority, worship, and regeneration form the essence of the unalterable gospel of Christ.

5. "We Affirm Together," 2nd paragraph.

preacher? And how shall they preach, except they are sent?" (Rom. 10:14-15). In the case of ECT, we are constrained to ask further, "And *what* will they believe if a Papist is sent?"

The authors state, "All who accept Christ as Lord and Saviour are brothers and sisters in Christ."[6] Wrong! Evangelicals often use such lingo, saying that someone has "accepted Christ as Saviour;" but biblical language is more precise. One suspects that the term *accept* was employed here precisely because of its widespread currency in evangelical circles; and because it is language acceptable to Papists.[7] The word *accept* here smacks of Pelagian evangelism, where a man's destiny is thought to rest with his own free will, if he will only "accept Christ." By contrast the scriptures speak of *saving faith* as trusting in Christ *alone* as he is offered in the gospel.[8]

Now, having provided a faulty description of *faith,* the ECT document uses this flawed premise to arrive at its definition of "brothers and sisters in Christ."[9]

ECT says, "As Evangelicals and Catholics, we dare not by needless and loveless conflict between ourselves give aid and comfort to enemies of the cause of Christ."[10] That remark overlooks the fact that Papistry is an enemy to the cause of Christ, and must be opposed. This truth was a fundamental principle of the Reformation, and evangelicals who sign a peace pact with Rome are aiding and abetting the Romish enemy of Christ.

The document expresses dismay over conflicts between evangelicals and Romanists in Latin American and Eastern Europe.[11] What is often the case, however, is that people in these regions are leaving Popery for other church affiliations; and that

---

6. "We Affirm Together," 3rd paragraph.

7. The language also provides comfort for nominal church-goers, who consider *historic faith* sufficient unto salvation.

8. See chapter 1 above.

9. "We Affirm Together," 3rd paragraph; "We Contend Together," 4th paragraph.

10. "Introduction," 9th paragraph.

11. "Introduction," 6th paragraph.

action might be a positive step, if they are doing so out of an expression of genuine faith and repentance.

Worship Issues

The subject of worship finds its way into the document only through the back door. ECT lists differences that are "frequently thought to divide us."[12] The list includes the following points: "Sacraments and ordinances as symbols of grace or as means of grace," "the Lord's Supper as eucharistic sacrifice or memorial meal," "remembrance of Mary and the saints or devotion to Mary and the saints," and "baptism as sacrament of regeneration or testimony to regeneration."[13] Here are clear allusions to Romish sacerdotalism, superstition, and the blasphemy of the Mass. Nevertheless, the presence of idolatry in Romish worship does not prevent the evangelical signatories from owning Rome as a true church, and Romish idolaters as brethren. By contrast, historic Protestants regularly exposed the corruptions and superstition of Romish worship, calling upon the practitioners of such idolatry to repent.[14]

Indeed, in view of the length of the ECT document, the subject of worship receives short shrift. Perhaps that's because evangelicals and Romanists are both attached to numerous man-made forms of worship. Since they share common presuppositions about the lawfulness of human innovations in worship, their dispute is merely over which outward forms of will worship are preferred. In other words, this is one area where the dispute really is a family feud. Historic Protestants find any form of extra-biblical worship

---

12. With this kind of language, perhaps the authors really believe that the Reformation was simply one giant *misunderstanding*. After all, are the issues enunciated really substantive? Are they issues that *actually do* divide, or are they simply issues merely *thought to* divide? Perhaps the Reformers were mistaken when they *thought* Papists were corrupting the gospel and resorting to idolatry, etc.

13. "We Search Together," 3rd paragraph.

14. See chapter 3 above.

unacceptable, regardless of whether it emanates from Rome or from American democratic impulses.

Church Issues

The language of ECT is clear; its signatories regard evangelicals and Roman Catholics as "brothers and sisters in Christ." They "affirm that opportunity and means for growth in Christian discipleship are available in our several communities."[15]

They go further: "The one Christ and one mission includes many other Christians, notably the Eastern Orthodox and those Protestants not commonly identified as Evangelical."[16] Are they talking about liberal Protestants here? If so, this is about the broadest definition of the church (and Christianity) one could devise. There is no discrimination between true and false churches, just as there is no discrimination between true and false gospels. All who merely profess some breed of nominal Trinitarianism are included in this ecumenical vision.

This concept is made painfully apparent by the inclusion of the Apostles' Creed as the only confessional formulation broad enough to encompass everyone they have invited to the ecumenical party.[17] It is true that during the Reformation both Protestants and Romanists affirmed their acceptance of the Apostles' Creed. Yet, writers on both sides contended over the proper meaning of the creed (for example, the expression "the holy catholic church"), just as they did so many other issues.[18] To include this creed, with no further explanation, is to render its use virtually meaningless.[19]

---

15. "We Affirm Together," 3rd paragraph; "We Contend Together," 4th paragraph; "We Witness Together, 5th paragraph.

16. "Introduction," 4th paragraph.

17. "We Affirm Together," 4th paragraph.

18. For example, Calvin follows the order of the Apostles' Creed in the *Institutes*; and the Confession of the English congregation at Geneva is structured upon the articles of the creed. Both Calvin and the Confession explain the creed, as a means of exposing Rome's departure from the ancient faith of the church.

19. William Cunningham illustrates the inadequacy of the Apostles' Creed to serve as a sufficient guard against heresy; see *Historical Theology* (1862;

Thirty years ago this kind of broad-church ecumenism would have been cried down among evangelicals as gross liberalism.

The ecumenical refrain builds as the document says, "Existing patterns of distrustful polemic and conflict are not the way [to unity]. We do know that God who has brought us into communion with himself through Christ intends that we also be in communion with one another."[20] Well, of course it follows that if Papists are in communion with God, and ought to be in communion with Protestants, there is an inescapable conclusion: why bother to evangelize Roman Catholics? Wouldn't that be a waste of time?[21] Of course it would: "it is neither theologically legitimate nor a prudent use of resources for one Christian commu-

---

rpt. Edinburgh: Banner of Truth, 1979), vol. 1, pp. 79-93. The ECT document is not itself a creed (or confession), in the classic sense of the term. A creed is an expression of doctrinal propositions, generally used to bear testimony to the truth, while excluding contrary doctrines and heretics from the community of the faithful. Creeds are founded upon the exposition of scripture. The ECT document studiously avoids making overt doctrinal statements, and does not even attempt any kind of systematic exposition of scripture from which to derive doctrinal propositions. After all, expounding the Bible might prove too divisive for their ecumenical efforts. There are a few scattered citations from scripture, along with the reference to the Apostles' Creed and quotations from the pope. While quotations by the pope may suffice for Romanists, it hardly commends the document to Protestants. Regarding ECT's use of the scriptures and the Apostles' Creed, perhaps ECT signatories hope to use them as a kind of incantation, which, if merely recited (without explanation), will mystically produce a grand reunion.

20. "We Hope Together," 4th paragraph.

21. Did our Protestant forefathers really waste a lot of time and effort – and some spill their blood – trying to reach Europe for Christ? The ECT document condemns the practice of proselytizing, or "sheep-stealing," which is defined as "recruiting people from another community for purposes of denominational or institutional aggrandizement" ("We Witness Together," 4th paragraph). It doesn't seem to occur to the authors that sectarian bias is not the only motivation for trying to persuade people to sever their ecclesiastical ties. It is a Christian duty to call men to repentance, exhorting them, for the sake of the gospel, to leave corrupt ecclesiastical communions.

nity to proselytize among active adherents of another Christian community."[22]

Extending this line of thinking, the document espouses a doctrine of individual sovereignty which serves as a further barrier against legitimate evangelism. "Those converted – whether understood as having received the new birth for the first time or as having experienced the reawakening of the new birth originally bestowed in the sacrament of baptism – must be given full freedom and respect as they discern and decide the community in which they will live their new life in Christ. In such discernment and decision, they are ultimately responsible to God and we dare not interfere with the exercise of that responsibility."[23] From the viewpoint of the ECT signatories, calling a Romanist to repentance would have to be considered undue interference.[24]

After quoting from 2 Corinthians 5:19, the document asserts: "To proclaim this Gospel and to sustain the community of the faith, worship, and discipleship that is gathered by this Gospel is the first and chief responsibility of the church."[25] But this asser-

22. A few lines later, the document adds: "Also to be rejected is the practice of comparing the strengths and ideals of one community with the weaknesses and failures of another" ("We Witness Together," 5th and 6th paragraphs).

In a related vein, the document says, "The decision of the committed Christian with respect to his communal allegiance and participation must be assiduously respected"("We Witness Together, 5th paragraph).

23. "We Witness Together," 8th paragraph.

24. Earlier the document states, "the decision of the committed Christian with respect to his communal allegiance must be assiduously respected." "Any form of coercion – physical, psychological, legal, economic – corrupts Christian witness and is to be unqualifiedly rejected" ("We Witness Together," 5th and 6th paragraphs). This is an interesting statement, since the Roman Catholic church has historically utilized the physical and legal persecution of Protestants, a trend which continues to this day in countries dominated by Popery. We are also curious: Would it be considered inappropriate to speak of hell, when exhorting a Romanist to repent – or would that fall under the prohibition against psychological manipulation?

25. "We Contend Together," 2nd paragraph.

tion begs the question: Which gospel will be preached? Which community of faith? Which means of worship?

The document lists among the unresolved differences between evangelicals and Roman Catholics, "the church as visible communion or invisible fellowship of true believers."[26] This is an interesting dilemma. The Reformers spoke of the church both in terms of a body not always visible to the eyes of men (i.e., the elect), as well as the true visible church; they made necessary distinctions when describing the relationships between these two perspectives. But in the ECT document we are given a choice of one or the other. Of course, Papists have often held that the identity of the church is equivalent to the institutional church of Rome; and perhaps some evangelicals (out of Anabaptist roots) see the church only in terms of an invisible spiritual body. But we stand firm with the formulations of the Protestant creeds and confessions (which mirror scriptures), sometimes speaking of the church as obscure to the eyes of men (the body of the elect), but at other times referring to the church in its institutional sense as an outward community of those professing the true religion (and their children).

Among the list of unresolved differences between evangelicals and Romanists is "the sole authority of Scripture (*sola scriptura*) or Scripture as authoritatively interpreted in the church."[27] This disagreement is the most fundamental issue of authority. Without agreement on this principle, all the talk of evangelistic zeal for the Christian mission is hollow.

ECT speaks of the obligation to contend "against all that opposes Christ and his cause."[28] Shouldn't that duty include contending against Roman Catholicism, since Rome promulgates a

---

26. "We Search Together," 3rd paragraph.

27. "We Search Together," 3rd paragraph. The ECT affirmation of the inspiration and infallibility of the scriptures is disingenuous, since Romanists and evangelicals do not hold to the same canon of scripture ("We Affirm together, 4th paragraph).

28. "We Contend Together," 1st paragraph.

false gospel and idolatry? If "earnestly contending for the faith" means anything (cf. Jude 3), surely it means that true believers must oppose those who corrupt the gospel and worship.

Evangelical Zeal?

Nowhere in the document is the term evangelical defined. We are told, however, that "the two communities in world Christianity that are most evangelistically assertive and most rapidly growing are Evangelicals and Catholics."[29] Apparently it's the *assertiveness* that's the essence of the evangelical spirit in view because, here again, we are not told which evangel is being promulgated. Indeed, it doesn't seem to matter which gospel is preached, as long as it is done earnestly.

The apostle Paul has warned us that there is "a zeal of God, but not according to knowledge" (Rom. 10:2). Based on the ECT document, one may easily perceive that there are both evangelicals and Roman Catholics who possess this unholy zeal.

29. "Introduction," 6th paragraph.

Chapter 7

Concluding Remarks

LET US RETURN for a moment to the early days of the apostolic church. The church was faced with controversy on account of the doctrine of the Judaizers.

The Judaizers held to an orthodox Christology; they believed in the inspiration and authority of the scriptures; they asserted the abiding validity of the moral law of God. Moreover, professing Christians were greatly outnumbered, living in a pagan society with a government that was hostile to biblical values. Based upon the worldly wisdom of ECT, the apostle Paul should have displayed unity with the Judaizers in order to "Christianize" the Roman Empire.

Instead, the apostle vehemently opposed the Judaizers. Why? The Judaizers upheld Old Testament ordinances, saying, "Except ye be circumcised after the manner of Moses, ye cannot be saved" (Acts 15:1). By making the ordinances into a work performed to obtain salvation, the Judaizers subverted the doctrine of salvation by grace. For that reason, the apostle exclaimed, "Behold, I Paul say unto you, that if ye be circumcised, Christ shall profit you nothing. For I testify again to every man that is circumcised, that he is a debtor to do the whole law. Christ is become of no effect unto you, whosoever of you are justified by the law; ye are fallen from grace" (Gal. 5:2-4).

In a parallel fashion, Catholicism has told its followers that "Except ye keep the doctrine and sacraments after the manner of Rome, ye cannot be saved." There is one notable difference: the Judaizers based their claim upon an erroneous understanding of scriptural ordinances, whereas Rome teaches its followers to rely upon a multitude of beliefs and practices which are nothing but "commandments and doctrines of men" (Col. 2:22; cf. Matt. 15:9; Mark 7:7).

Thus, to Roman Catholics who may read this publication, we call upon you to repent from any reliance upon Romish ordinances; for Christ will become of no effect to you if you resort to these ordinances as a basis for salvation. True salvation comes through resting in Christ alone; it is all of grace, or not at all. "Salvation is of the Lord" (Jonah 2:9). The true people of God forsake all hope of salvation in any source but Christ alone.

Christians are also commanded to forsake idolatry. That is a principal reason why repentant sinners must leave Rome. The worship of Roman Catholicism is, in large measure, institutionalized superstition and idolatry; and believers must flee from the presence of such corrupt worship. "What concord hath Christ with Belial? or what part hath he that believeth with an infidel? And what agreement hath the temple of God with idols? for ye are the temple of the living God; as God hath said, I will dwell in them, and walk in them; and I will be their God, and they shall be my people. Wherefore come out from among them, and be ye separate, saith the Lord, and touch not the unclean thing; and I will receive you, and will be a Father unto you, and ye shall be my sons and daughters, saith the Lord Almighty" (2 Cor. 6:15-18).

To evangelicals who read this booklet, we offer a solemn warning. You may hold to an orthodox Christology, the inspiration of the scriptures, a biblical morality: and yet, even with all these convictions, you still may be in need of salvation.

If you are resting your assurance of salvation upon your "decision;" if you think that your "free will" or "accepting Christ" produced the new birth within you; then you are deceived – you are no better off than a Judaizer or a Romanist. You have made your "decision" into a work, and subverted the doctrine of salvation by grace.

We showed earlier that faith is merely the instrument, not the ground of salvation. Sadly, we have seen multitudes among evangelicals who have distorted the role of faith, or redefined the term *faith* so as to nullify its biblical meaning. To any who are subject to such "evangelical" delusions regarding faith, we cry again, "Repent." Come to Christ in genuine faith, resting in him alone, as he is offered in the gospel. "Him hath God exalted with his right hand to be a Prince and a Saviour, for to give repentance to Israel, and forgiveness of sins" (Acts 5:31).

To any evangelicals who have signed or supported the ECT accord, we have but one thing to say: Repent! The ECT document was bad enough. But, quite frankly, we find some of the rationale offered for its support as troubling (or more so) than the accord itself.[1] The apostle Paul is emphatic, "Though we, or an angel from heaven, preach any other gospel unto you than that which we have preached unto you, let him be accursed." Hey! in case you missed the point, the apostle repeats it again in the next verse: "As we said before, so say I now again, If any man preach any other gospel unto you than that ye have received, let him be accursed" (Gal. 1:8-9).

In light of the apostle's admonition – and in view of Rome's perversion of the gospel – it is absolutely inexcusable for any professing Protestant to lend support to the ECT document, which

1. For example, see J. I. Packer's defensive article, "Why I Signed It," *Christianity Today,* December 12, 1994 (vol. 38, no. 14), pp. 34-37. Packer has the audacity to say that "differences about salvation and the church should not hinder them [evangelicals and Roman Catholics] from joint action to re-Christianize the North American milieu." Quite frankly, we are skeptical that society can be truly "Christianized" apart from a proper view of salvation and the church.

Packer goes on to laud joint "mission ventures that involve evangelicals and Catholics side by side." He cites examples, including "Billy Graham's cooperative evangelism, in which all the churches in an area, of whatever stripe, are invited to share." He also mentions, "charismatic get-togethers, some of them one-off, some of them regular, and some of them huge, where the distinction between Protestant and Catholic vanish in a Christ-centered unity of experience." These items which Packer views as positive developments we regard as ominous signs of the apostasy of our times. In chapter 2

speaks of a common mission with Rome. Those who are leaders among the people bear a special responsibility in this regard: "My brethren, be not many masters, knowing that we shall receive the greater condemnation [*judgment*]" (James 3:1).[2]

We have a particular concern for those who profess to be Reformed in their theology. For too long the Reformed community has winked at the heresies of the broader evangelical community; now the ECT accord has presented a new level of toleration. The apostle's rebuke to the Corinthians is entirely appropriate for the present climate of toleration in Reformed churches: "But I fear, lest by any means, as the serpent beguiled Eve through his subtilty, so your minds should be corrupted from the simplicity that is in Christ. For if he that cometh preacheth another Jesus, whom we have not preached, or if ye receive another spirit, which ye have not received, or another gospel, which ye have not accepted, ye might well bear with him" (2 Cor. 11:3-4).

It is past time for Reformed Protestants to face up to the sin of ungodly toleration. We have tolerated the false gospels, the false Christs, and the false worship of the broader evangelical community. Some "Reformed" denominations have openly embraced the Pelagian evangelistic methodology and the will-worship of evangelicalism. "Remember therefore from whence thou art fallen, and

---

above, we noted the heretical nature of Graham's decisionalism; and the participation of Roman Catholics in the "follow-up" to a Graham crusade only confirms our opinion that these rallies are fatally flawed. Space does not permit us to provide an analysis of the charismatic movement; but we emphatically deny that the emotional atmosphere of these "get-togethers" should be labelled a "Christ-centered unity of experience."

2. Church leaders who signed the ECT document should not be exempt from criticism, regardless of their stature as churchmen. After all the apostle Paul says, "Them that sin rebuke before all, that others also may fear" (1 Tim. 5:20).

One of the biggest supporters of ECT is Charles Colson. For a succinct analysis of Colson's theology, see "The Counterfeit Faith of Charles Colson," by John W. Robbins; published in *The Trinity Review*, January and February 1994 (P.O. Box 1666, Hobbs, N.M. 88240).

repent, and do the first works: or else I will come unto thee quickly, and will remove thy candlestick out of his place, except thou repent" (Rev. 2:5).

Living in an era of religious pluralism, we are too apt to forget that heresy is a form of *moral corruption;* it is classed among "works of the flesh" along with adultery, fornication, uncleanness, idolatry, witchcraft, murder, and drunkenness (Gal. 5:19-21). That's how the Lord views heresy. And thus heresy is *dangerous* to our souls; there are heresies which are "damnable" in their nature (2 Pet. 2:1).

The issues which fostered the Protestant Reformation are not simply matters for academic debate. They are great and eternal matters respecting the way of salvation and the proper worship of God.

Bibliography

Ankerberg, John and John Weldon. *Protestants and Catholics: Do They Now Agree?* Eugene, Oregon: Harvest House, 1995. This book suffers from decisionalism and other errors of contemporary evangelicalism; the volume contains specific criticisms of ECT, and useful observations about the heresies of Rome.

Armstrong, John (ed.) *Roman Catholicism: Evangelicals Analyze What Divides and Unites Us.* Chicago: Moody Press, 1994. An important book, but some of the contributors are far too conciliatory toward Rome. The best essays are: "Did I Really Leave the Holy Catholic Church?" by William Webseter, "The Evangelical Moment?" by John Armstrong, "What Really Caused the Great Divide?" by W. Robert Godfrey, and "What Still Keeps Us Apart?" by Michael Horton.

Beeke, Joel. "Justification by Faith Alone (The Relation of Faith to Justification)," in *Justification by Faith Alone* (edited by Don Kistler; Morgan, Pa.: Soli Deo Gloria, 1994), pp. 53-105.

Belgic Confession of Faith (1561). Available in many books, including Schaff's *Creeds of Christendom.*

Bennett, Richard. *We Ought to Obey God Rather Than Men.* A brief analysis of ECT document. Formerly a Roman Catholic priest, Bennett has many publications which expose the evils of Romish doctrine and practice. Write to: Berean Beacon, P. O. Box 55353, Portland, Oregon 97238

Buchanan, James. *The Doctrine of Justification: An Outline of Its History in the Church and of Its Exposition from Scripture.* Edinburgh, 1867. Various reprints have been done, the most recent from Banner of Truth.

Calvin, John. *Acts of the Council of Trent: with the Antidote* [1547]. A thorough Protestant analysis of official Roman Catholic dogma. It is included in vol. 3 of the *Selected Works of John Calvin* (edited and translated by Henry Beveridge). 1851; rpt. Grand Rapids: Baker, 1983.

Calvin, John. *The Necessity of Reforming the Church.* 1544; rpt. Dallas: Protestant Heritage Press, 1995. This tract contains important comments about true worship.

Calvin, John. *Reply by John Calvin to Letter by Cardinal Sadolet to the Senate and People of Geneva.* A concise historic statement of the differences between Rome and Protestants on the subject of justification. It is included in vol. 1 of the *Selected Works of John Calvin* (edited and translated by Henry Beveridge). 1844; rpt. Grand Rapids: Baker, 1983.

Chemnitz, Martin. *Examination of the Council of Trent* [1565-73]. Translated by Fred Kramer, 4 vols. St Louis: Concordia, 1971-86). A comprehensive Lutheran analysis of official Roman Catholic dogma.

Clarkson, David. *Practical Works.* 1865; rpt. Edinburgh: Banner of Truth, 1988). Volume 3 contains Clarkson's sermon on public worship, and a book on the practical evils of Popery.

Confession of the English Congregation at Geneva (1556). Available in a loose-leaf reprint of *The Genevan Book of Order: The Form of Prayers and Ministration of the Sacraments, etc., Used in the English Congregation at Geneva.* Dallas: Presbyterian Heritage, 1993.

Cunningham, William. *Discussions on Church Principles: Popish, Erastian, and Presbyterian.* 1863; rpt. Edmonton: Still Waters, 1991. Contains many excellent essays.

Cunningham, William. *Historical Theology.* 1862; rpt. Edinburgh: Banner of Truth, 1979. Of great usefulness, especially the section on justification and the discussion on images and icons.

Eire, Carlos M. N. *War Against the Idols: The Reformation of Worship from Erasmus to Calvin.* Cambridge Univ. Press, 1986). A detailed and scholarly history, showing that the struggle against corrupt worship was a central tenet of the Reformation.

Foxe, John. *Acts and Monuments....* (First published in 1563, and commonly known as the *Foxe's Book of Martyrs.*) We insert this entry into our bibliography, lest readers become lulled into false optimism by the siren song of modern toleration. The painful reality of Rome's historic hostility to the gospel, coupled with the faithful testimony of the martyrs, should keep us ever vigilant to earnestly contend for the faith.

French Confession of Faith (1559). Available in many books, including Schaff's *Creeds of Christendom.*

Gerstner, John H. "The Theological Boundaries of Evangelical Faith," in *The Evangelicals: What They Believe, Who They Are, Where They Are Changing* (edited by David F. Wells and John D. Woodbridge; Nashville: Abingdon, 1975).

Heidelberg Catechism (1563). Available in many books, including Schaff's *Creeds of Christendom.*

Hunt, Dave. *A Woman Rides the Beast.* An exposé of Rome and the ECT document. Unfortunately, the book is tainted by the author's adherence to dispensationalism.

Kistler, Don (ed.). *Justification by Faith Alone.* Morgan, Pa.: Soli Deo Gloria, 1994. The articles in this book are of mixed quality. All authors did not stick to their specific topics, with the result that the volume as a whole contains much repetition. By far, the best essay is Joel Beeke's discussion on the role of faith in justification.

Knox, John. *Selected Writings: Public Epistles, Treatises, and Expositions to the Year 1559.* Dallas: Presbyterian Heritage, 1995. Of special importance are Knox's pointed statements on worship, contained in the first 100 pages of this volume.

Luther, Martin. *The Bondage of the Will.* Translated by J. I. Packer and O. R. Johnston. 1525; rpt. London: James Clarke, 1957.

MacArthur, John. *Reckless Faith: When the Church Loses Its Will To Discern.* Wheaton: Crossway Books, 1994. Contains a special chapter on the ECT document.

Manton, Thomas. *A Body of Divinity.* 1692; rpt. Edinburgh: Banner of Truth, 1992). A good primer on theology, following the contents of the Westminster Shorter Catechism.

Reed, Kevin. *Biblical Church Government.* Dallas: Presbyterian Heritage Publications, 1983, 1994 (expanded edition). A brief statement of scriptural principles of church polity.

Reed, Kevin. *Biblical Worship.* Dallas: Presbyterian Heritage, 1995. A brief examination of the scriptural principles of worship.

Reisinger, Ernest C. *What Should We Think of the Carnal Christian?* Edinburgh: Banner of Truth, 1978. A refutation of false doctrine of the carnal Christian.

Schaff, Philip. *The Creeds of Christendom.* 1931 (6th edition); rpt. Grand Rapids: Baker, 1983), 3 vols. A standard reference; enables readers to examine the full text of creeds, both Romish and Protestant.

Second Helvetic Confession (1566). The most widely available English translation is found in Schaff's, *Creeds of Christendom.*

Scottish Confession of Faith (1560). Available in various editions.

Westminster Confession of Faith, Larger and Shorter Catechisms (1647-48). Reprinted in many sources, although the best edition currently in print is produced by the Free Presbyterian Church of Scotland.

Wiley, James A. *The History of Protestantism.* London, 1874-77. A 3-volume history, sometimes reprinted.

Wiley, James A. *The Papacy: Its History, Dogmas, Genius, and Prospects.* London, 1867. An exposé on the history and dogmas of the papacy.

Scripture Index

Subject Index